HOW TO
TOP EXAMS & ENJOY STUDIES
STUDY TECHNIQUES FOR EVERY STUDENT

HOW TO
TOP EXAMS &
ENJOY STUDIES

STUDY TECHNIQUES FOR EVERY STUDENT

Dhaval Bathia

JAICO PUBLISHING HOUSE

Mumbai Delhi Bangalore Kolkata
Hyderabad Chennai Ahmedabad Bhopal

Published by Jaico Publishing House
121 Mahatma Gandhi Road
Mumbai - 400 001
jaicopub@vsnl.com
www.jaicobooks.com

HOW TO TOP EXAMS & ENJOY STUDIES
ISBN 81-7992-133-6

First Jaico Impression: 2003
Sixteenth Jaico Impression: 2008

Printed by
Sanman & Co.
113, Shivshakti Ind. Estate, Marol Naka
Andheri (E), Mumbai - 400 059.

DEDICATION

This book is dedicated to the oyster. An oyster is a small mollusk that lives in the sea. It has the miraculous ability of turning a grain of sand into a shining, sparkling pearl. A grain of sand in the shell is an irritant to the oyster. So, in order to get rid of the grain of sand, the oyster starts secreting a special enzyme. It keeps on secreting the enzyme until the grain of sand becomes a pearl! The question in our mind is what is it that changes the most abundant, the cheapest and the most ignored thing (a grain of sand) into a rare, expensive and sought-after thing (a pearl)?

Is secreting an enzyme like an act of spitting? Partly, Yes. But it is really the undivided focused attention of the oyster to get rid of the obstacle that enables it to make this transformation. It involves itself in a continuous, non-stop activity until it gets rid of the grain of sand.

The lesson that we learn is that in the quest of removing the obstacles from our lives, we can make something more beautiful. Our greatest liabilities become our greatest assets.

'IF you cannot remove obstacles from your life, Learn to make something more beautiful (more productive) out of it.'

When Michelangelo is walking on the road, he sees a stone in front of him. This is an obstacle for the layman. But, Michelangelo takes a chisel and a hammer and makes a beautiful sculpture of David out of the same stone.

This attempt is dedicated to my parents and my sister for inspiring me to discover the David in me.

❑❑

CONTENTS

PREFACE

Hard work is certainly the key to success. You must be ready to put in efforts to enjoy the fruits of life. Some people do not put in efforts when they are in school or college. They waste their lives. Later in life they repent not having worked hard. There is no substitute for hard work. It is a must. But, in today's competitive world, hard work alone is not enough. The number of educated job-seekers is increasing on the one hand and on the other, jobs are not increasing as much. In fact, many people are losing their jobs due to automation. Thus, apart from working hard, we need to become smart. 'SMART-WORK' is as vital as hard work to win in life. Think of a woman stitching clothes by hand and another using a sewing machine. One is working hard and the other is working smart. Who puts up a better performance? Obviously, the woman with a sewing machine is able to put up a better performance. The woman uses technology. She takes advantage of scientific advancement. Similarly, there are sciences that relate to the human brain. They help us understand the functions and features of our brain. If we learn from these sciences, we can be successful in our work. This is true smartness. I will introduce you to the various sciences of the human brain that can help you become successful in your work. They help us to make hard work easier.

I never scored exceptionally good marks in school or college, but I have always been a very good student. Mainly because my interest was not only in academics, but also in sports, games, co-curricular and extra-curricular activities. Thus, I was a competent all-rounder doing very well in school and college. I always wanted to be smart rather than only be a hard worker. Hard work when combined with smartness gets the best results.

Some years back, I saw a young child on stage throwing a challenge to the audience. His challenge was that if you gave him any date from 1st January 1995 to 31st December 2000, he would tell you the day on which that date fell. I was simply amazed by the way he did it. Suppose you asked him what the day on 14th September 2000 was, he would tell you in 5 seconds that it was a Thursday. He could tell you the day on which any date fell on any year between 1995 and 2000. Another thing that inspired me about the boy was his age. He was just 8 years old. I thought that if he could do it, why couldn't I? So, I started researching information on calculating dates and other related things. After a lot of research, I devised many techniques that would help me do it. But, I also came across many other books and on reading them I learnt about some related issues. I even developed my own techniques. I tried to apply them while studying my own textbooks. They did prove effective. They did not improve my marks to a very great extent. There was some increase in my marks. But, I realised that I was putting in less effort and my task had become much easier and simpler than before.

After a few months of practice, I was able to calculate very fast and even my memory had become very sharp. Whenever I was with my friends or relatives, I used to demonstrate to them my various techniques and stunts. Many of them suggested that I do it professionally. It was then that I started giving demonstrations, and holding seminars and workshops in schools and colleges. The reason was that I wanted to share my knowledge with others. Now, I have written this book for you. In it I have mentioned various memory techniques and methods to calculate fast. Since this book was written for a specific age group, I could not mention all the matter that I know. In future I will include other techniques.

When I first thought of writing this book, I wanted to mention only those techniques that would help students increase their brainpower. But someone suggested that it could be a guidebook for the students. Thus, to make the book complete and comprehensive, I included topics like sub-conscious study and Time Management'.

I have written this book in such a form that it would help all readers. The memory techniques in this book will help students and others. The basics of speed mathematics which will help students and others calculate faster. Sub-conscious study and visualisation will also be useful to many different readers. FRT can be a very useful tool for people like me who are unable to spend long hours on studies.

I have kept the book short and specific. If you cannot understand something, don't jump ahead. If you do so, you will not understand what is being taught next. Go slowly and if you do not understand something, go over it again.

I have not given commonly known advice such as that students must not omit any questions in the paper, or they must not watch TV while studying, and must not eat too much oily food, etc. I assume that the reader knows these things.

I have used the masculine gender throughout the book.

You can mail me your suggestions at:
memoryexpert@rediffmail.com

There are certain quotes, poems and articles attributed to 'anonymous' simply because the source from which I took that line or quote had the word 'anonymous'. If you know the author, please let me know.

ABOUT THE AUTHOR

Dhaval Bathia is a 19-year-old student. This is his first book. He studies commerce at the Narsee Monjee College in Mumbai. He won 'The Best Student of the Year Award' in his college in 2000-01. He is an active member of the inter-collegiate cultural event 'UMANG'. He plays chess at the metropolitan level.

Dhaval is also studying company secretaryship and finance. He conducts workshops and seminars in the field of Vedic mathematics, memory power et al. He is a practitioner of Reiki and uses his spiritual knowledge as an integral part of his daily work, which includes self-hypnosis, inner mind assertion, visualization, meditation and sub-conscious powers.

He has conducted workshops for schools, colleges and coaching classes all over the country. He also conducts workshops on 'corporate memory' and his clientele includes a number of leading companies.

He has won many awards in oratory and literary competitions at urban and even at state level.

Dhaval edits an online newsletter called *Smart Ideas* which has a large global subscription base.

Dhaval is one of the members of the Blue Ribbon Movement which is an NGO working for a better India.

He is a visiting lecturer in many professional institutes. Dhaval is one of the world's youngest faculties for management students and has taught mathematics to many MBA students. His articles have appeared in a number of newspapers and magazines. He writes regularly for different websites.

He is a computer programmer and runs, along with his father and uncle, a finance and investment portal called www.envestindia.com

You can write to him at memoryexpert@rediffmail.com

ACKNOWLEDGEMENTS

Thanks to Mummy and Daddy for all the love, support and caring. To my sister for being a great inspiration. To my uncles, aunties and cousins for always being there. I am indebted to my grandmother for telling me life-changing stories and inspiring ideas right from a very early age.

Thanks to Pratik Sonawala who stands as an example to me. He works with unlimited energy.

To Shirishuncle, Jyotiaunty and Brinda for their support.

To my uncles Shailesh and Pankaj for their wisdom.

To Anand, Janak and Haseet for their tips.

To Reuben, Kanwardeep, Rishi, Abhishek, Hemang, Prashant, Kunal, Nainil for giving me so much in life. To Usha Aunty for attuning me to abundance.

To Harjeet and Mahek who are living examples of the techniques mentioned in this book.

To Father Ernest Fernandes, Father Clifton Lobo, Father Ronnie Braganza and Father Francis Carvalho for their motivation.

To my teachers at St. Anne's. They taught me the English language. I come from a Gujarati background. They have always been a source of strength throughout my school career. This book is specially dedicated to them.

I thank my principal Prof. M.K. Desai for his support and interest.

I would like to thank my professors at Narsee Monjee College. They have helped me achieve both academically and otherwise. They are the people who have made N. M. one of the best commercial educational institutes in India.

To my friends at the Blue Ribbon Movement, UMANG and Computer Society.

I would like to thank a lot of people who have indirectly helped me. First of all I thank Mr. S.K.Sachdeva for his motivating articles in CSR. I also thank Dilip Thakore of *Education World* for bringing to us such a wonderful magazine regularly.

I also thank the people at egurucool.com for creating such a wonderful portal which I regularly surf and also Jhumur and Vinita from *Education Times* for their support.

I express my sincere gratitude to the PTA members, principals of different schools and colleges, proprietors of coaching classes, and of Management Institutes, HRD personnel in corporate houses and my students all across the country for being a great inspiration for my seminars.

I thank the team of my publishers for their advice and experience.

A lot of thanks to friends, well-wishers, relatives and colleagues. Especially the rank-holders of N.M. College for their unconditional support. Without them, this book would not have been possible.

1. HOW TO CONCENTRATE

As a child I read the story of sailors stranded on an island. The ocean provided them food but they needed fire to cook the fish they caught. Also, the fire and its smoke would be seen by a ship which would then come to their rescue. But however hard they tried, the crew could not find a way to light a fire. Three days passed by and they could not think of any way to light fire. Suddenly, on the fourth morning, the captain thought of a brilliant idea. He broke open his watch and removed the glass surface. This glass surface of the watch was used as a lens to converge the rays of the sun to produce fire. He concentrated the rays of the sun on thin, dry twigs of wood and made fire. The captain had realised that the individual rays of the sun could not ignite wood but if they were focused at one point, they could.

Now, you may ask me what do we learn from the story?

The lesson we learn is that concentration is a very powerful tool to achieve results. The captain concentrated the rays of the sun using a convex lens. The individual rays could not have created a fire but when concentrated they produced fire!

Concentration is the accumulation of scattered elements.

Scientists know that laser is a weak source of energy but the same laser if focused properly can drill a hole in a diamond which is the world's hardest substance.

James Conant says that generals who scatter their armies in the battlefield are almost sure to lose. They must concentrate their armies to face an attack.

Focus and concentration are related ideas. Scattered clouds of steam rise upwards in the sky. They are powerless and unable to accomplish anything. These same clouds when concentrated and condensed in a steam boiler, can cut through solid rock and even propel atomic ships.

Mahabharata tells us the story of Arjun's lesson in archery. Arjun and other pupils were asked to hit the eye of a wooden bird placed in a tree. As each student took aim, the teacher Dronachary asked him what he could see. All other pupils described what they could see – the leaves of the tree, the sky beyond and so on – and all missed. Arjun replied, 'I see the eye of the bird.' He hit the target.

Concentration is a powerful factor that determines whether a person will be successful in his work. In discussions with friends and colleagues, many have asked me how they should concentrate in their studies. In this chapter, I have discussed various methods by which a person can enhance his concentration.

Given below are some ways in which you can increase your ability to focus your thoughts, your energy and time for a particular purpose. There are many factors that contribute to it like the right place and time, creating interest, meditation, etc.

PLACE AND TIME

As far as possible, try to have one place and time for study. Avoid doing any other work at that place and at that time. The reason is that when we use the same place for studies regularly, our mind accepts the fact that that particular place is meant for attentive and serious work. Thus, whenever we sit at that place our concentration improves. This is a form of autosuggestion. The place where you regularly sit will acquire a sacredness of its own as the place for serious work.

You can arrange your books, stationery etc. at this place. Try to keep away all those things that cause distraction such as, a hand-held video game, a comic book etc. If you are a believer, you can place an image of a deity in your study area.

Your chair should be comfortable. You should relax yourself completely. If you are not comfortable, you will not be able to concentrate. The base of your spine needs rest after long hours of work, and it should have support while studying.

The best time to study is early morning. There are two reasons for it. The first reason is that you are fresh in the morning after having had a good night's sleep. Early in the morning, our emotions do not affect our studies. We are fresh. When we study in the evening, our mind constantly remembers whatever has happened throughout the day. We think over all the incidents that took place right from the time we got up. A few years back, I had the habit of studying late in the evening and in the night. But, what I observed was that in the night my mind used to be dominated by emotions. Sometimes, if I had had a fight or a quarrel with a friend during the day, I would think over the incident again and again. If something very nice happened during the day, I would think of it to relive the pleasure. If I had done something wrong, feelings of guilt or fear would dominate me so powerfully that even though my book would be open, I could not read. I know of a man who is so fond of baseball that whenever his home-team lost an important match, he got so frustrated that he was unable to do any work for the rest of that day.

Obviously, this frustration lasts only for a day. The next morning, he is back to normal. Thus, it is advisable to study early in the morning, when no happy or sad incident for the day has taken place because *each incident leaves behind memories and emotions on which we would like to ponder again and again; obviously leading to a loss of concentration.* So, preferably study in the morning.

The second reason why it is advisable to study early in the morning is that the environment is silent and it helps you to concentrate.

In the ancient Vedic school of India, the pupils used to get up before sunrise and in the silence of dawn, there used to be a transfer of knowledge from the teacher to the disciple. This system of learning produced some of the biggest discoveries and inventions in mathematics, sciences, astronomy, medicine, astrology, spiritualism and a host of other subjects.

3

You will find that whatever is studied for one hour early in the morning is always remembered better than anything studied during one hour at any other time of the day.

Dr. Babasaheb Ambedkar led the team that framed the Constitution of India. He was a politician and social reformer. He came from a very poor family. He often, went hungry to buy books. When he was young, he lived in a small congested neighbourhood. He needed to get up earlier to be able to study. His ability to concentrate reached such levels that no amount of external disturbance could make any difference to him. He could achieve concentration while in a bus, train or a room filled with people.

Thus, the best time to study is early in the morning when you are not feeling sleepy or drowsy. Forcing your brain to study when you are feeling sleepy is useless. The second best time to study is according to your biorhythms.

Vladimir Kramnik was crowned the world champion of chess when he defeated Gary Kasparov. Kramnik remarked that he played chess very well during the nighttime. He is at his best during the night. According to him, if world championships were played at night, he would have been a world champion much earlier.

Each of us has a time of the day when we perform our best. Any work that is done at that time yields the best results. This is called, in scientific language, 'biorhythms.'

Observe yourself for a few days. You will find that there are specific times of the day when you work well. It may be in the evening or late at night. Any work done during that time produces the best results. I do any work that requires concentration and thinking early in the morning. I write my book early in the morning. This time helps me to think and generate some of the best ideas.

Each one of us has a biorhythm that remains constant over time. If you work well during evening, you will always work well in the evening. It does not change frequently. It is uniform.

Even nature has its own biorhythm. Flowers bloom only dur-

4

ing spring every year; trees shed leaves only in a specific season every year. The seasons follow one another in a rhythmic pattern. Thus, observe your own rhythmic patterns. Find out the time when you perform best and work accordingly. You will be amazed to see the improvement in your performance.

INTEREST

We love doing those things in which we are interested. These things do not appear as work for us. We can easily concentrate on them. Similarly, we must understand the importance of education. We cannot do without education in the modern world. As we grow, we become more and more concerned about our studies and concentration comes automatically. Haribhai Kothari is a well-known social reformer and thinker of India. He once said that there are three types of people on a beach. The first category consists of people who loiter around the shore. These people get only the seashells and sand. The second category of people are the ones who go into shallow waters and get fish. The third category of people are the ones who go into the deep ocean bed and these are the ones who get pearls out of the sea.

Similarly, there are three categories of students too. Some students treat their books and studies casually. These students get the shells and sand. Some students study the subject with a little more interest and they get the fish, while those who study the subject with enthusiasm and passion get the pearls. When you study your subject matter with interest and enthusiasm, you will get the best out of it.

There was a time when one scholar would ask another, "Have you **studied** that book?" Then came a time when the question was reframed, "Have you **read** that book?" Now one asks, "Have you **seen** that book?"

Our duty is not to read, but to study deeply. Only when you study **in depth** and go to the core of it, you get the **pearls**.

Two students read from the same textbook, give the same exam and study roughly for the same length of time. But still, one student gets an A+ while the other manages to get a C. The main difference is that one student studied the book and the other student simply read it.

Go to the core, to the depth and you will get the pearls.

CHANGE OF AIR

I always recommend having a picture of a natural landscape in front of your eyes when you sit at your desk. Use such a picture instead of the poster of your favourite superstar. The superstar's poster can be stuck elsewhere. Blue and green are colours soothing to your eyes. Red, orange and other bright colours can agitate you. Get a good picture of a natural landscape and keep it at eye-level, it will fill you with freshness and calm.

Many students resort to drinking tea when they study for long hours. It is their belief that a cup of tea will enhance their concentration and remove their drowsiness. This belief may be true, but see to it that you stay away from this habit. It is always better not to get addicted to anything. If you are addicted, when you do not get a cup of tea, you develop a headache and cannot work.

For longer periods of study, we get bored sitting in the same place. Sometimes, students get so frustrated, that they just feel like throwing away their books and running away. Such frustration is caused by excessive studies and naturally leads to a loss of concentration. The remedy is to spend some time in a natural environment. It could be anything that can give you fresh air. It could be your lawn; a garden (if it is nearby) or the best solution is the terrace of your apartment. Sitting in your room for a long time makes you feel as if you are sitting in a prison and thus change of air is absolutely necessary. Fresh air will recharge the batteries of your mind.

URGENCY STAGE

During stages of urgency, our ability to focus on anything increases. I know of many students who study just a day before the examination, and with an amazing amount of concentration. Remember, that these states of urgency are like 'do or die' situations when you have to concentrate. Students find that during such states of urgency they can grasp a large amount of subject matter, which would otherwise take much longer to study. The feeling that it is a must-do activity increases our concentration.

I use the countdown system of time-management. On a piece of paper, I write the number of days left before the deadline. For example, if I have one month I write down a big 30 and look at it for a minute. The next day, I rub off the 30 and write 29. And the next day, I rub off 29 and write 28. As each day passes, I sense a feeling of urgency that triggers concentration. If I miss a day of studies, it gives me a sense of guilt. I try to make up for lost time by working longer the next day. You can try the same thing, especially for an examination. As each day passes, you will concentrate more and more. Ten, nine, eight, seven... The countdown system eliminates any nervousness on your part. Nervousness arises due to lack of practice and effort. When you open your book at the last minute, you feel tense and nervous because you have little time and a lot to study. This leads to panic. When you use the countdown system, you have been *increasing your efforts at a steady pace day after day.* You will not get nervous but instead be mentally prepared for the examination.

REREADING

Sometimes, we find that we are not able to concentrate no matter however hard we try. The subject matter bounces over our head and in spite of many attempts we are unable to understand. Don't try to force yourself. Just read your subject matter once or twice, if you understand it, well and good. Take every line slowly, word by word. Even if it takes you half an hour to learn one paragraph, there is no problem. Try to understand as much as possible and simply forget the rest. Read the same matter after two days and see the difference for yourself. You will be surprised to find how well you can understand it now. The second time always works. The third attempt will make you even better.

When you read the text for the first time, it is so new to you that you cannot comprehend it. The words seem alien and you cannot understand the meaning. Now, your subconscious mind understands the problem and tries to find a solution. So, wait for a couple of days and then study again. By doing so, you give enough time to your subconscious mind to make the matter clear for you. (Refer to the chapter 9 on Subconscious study.)

MEDITATION

Try this experiment for yourself. Put a coin in a bucket of water. Swirl the water with your hand and then try to see whether the coin shows heads or tails. Try to determine its features. You will find that it is impossible to tell the features of the coin when the water is disturbed. Once the water settles down, look at the coin again. Now you can see it clearly. This example teaches us to calm down, to relax, and to be still. Whenever we sit down to study, there are thousands of thoughts in our brains. We want to watch TV, read novels, surf the net, talk to friends, listen to music, etc. All these thoughts are disturbances in our mind. They do not allow the lesson to penetrate the brain. You can only concentrate by calming down the ripples. This is the power of stillness. On a still surface of water, even the tiny granule of sand will create a ripple but when the water is disturbed no matter how many rocks you throw in it, there is no effect. Our lifestyle is such that people suffer stress everywhere and so the important thing is to calm down. To be still. To relax. And the best way to do it is by **meditating.**

For 'natural' meditation, relax yourself in your chair. Close your eyes and try to be still. Take a deep breath. Imagine yourself in a natural environment. A beautiful natural landscape full of flowers in blossom. See yourself as a river springing from the mountain and then flowing through the land. See yourself flowing down a waterfall. Imagine yourself diving in a blue pond. Try to imagine a variety of colourful fishes. Then suddenly it starts raining, the environment comes alive. You become completely fresh and relaxed. All your fears, tensions, anxieties, worries, stress have disappeared. You feel energetic and alive. The rain stops. You see a rabbit running down the lush green meadow. Two shy squirrels eating nuts on the branch of a tree. The sun shines brightly again. Fill the picture, or the movie, with beautiful colours and live images. Paint life into every creature. See the butterfly among flowers, or the arch of the rainbow in the sky, the smiles of daffodils and the cow in the meadow. You can take a dip in the cool waters of the sea. See the aquatic world in all its beautiful forms. Enjoy this experience for a short while and then slowly open your eyes. Pray for a short while and ask God to help you in your work. Start your work.

You should meditate for around five minutes daily before studying. Let your imagination run wild. It will calm all your thoughts and you will easily understand what you read.

You must have realised that while you were reading the words — calm, relax, silent, blue pond, petals, rainbow, meadow etc. — in the above paragraph it created a feeling of silence in you. If just reading the words was powerful enough to calm you down, you can imagine how powerful the impact will be when you actually sit at your table, close your eyes and see the picture for yourself. Whenever you are feeling frustrated, repeat the words 'RELAX', 'CALM DOWN', again and again and see the difference for yourself.

One of my friends told me about an article that he had read in a magazine. The article mentioned an American principal and how he changed a bunch of rowdies in his school. There was a group of students in his school and not a single one of them would study. They used to chew chewing gum the whole day long, play basketball, listen to music, and loiter around. Their life was very unproductive. The principal saw that day-by-day their grades were becoming worse. He hit upon an idea.

He hired a chess coach for his school and he started teaching chess to the students. Somehow he was able to create enthusiasm for the game amongst the boys. They practised chess regularly for many days. They held friendly competitions amongst themselves on weekends. As time

9

passed, the teachers in the school observed that the students were able to concentrate more on their work. Chess is a game that requires serious and concentrated thinking. It left an impact on the students. Earlier, they would not to sit in one place for a long time. After learning chess, their attention to a specific act or work increased sharply. The parents were happy to see an improvement in their academic performance.

I play chess for my college and we are one of the best teams in the city. Believe me, I have never seen an active player of chess do badly in his work. The game makes you sit in one place, be patient and think. This is the first requirement for success—the ability to be patient and think.

I suggest to parents that if they think their children cannot concentrate on anything for long hours, then make sure that you teach them chess. This is a common problem. Parents complain that their children do not focus on any particular activity. They have restless minds which do not settle down to any particular activity. If this is your problem, then you can adopt the method that the American high school principal adopted and that is to teach your child the game of chess.

MUSIC

If you use music for studies, make sure that you use one without words. **Words trigger images in our mind** and the images take our concentration away from our work. Musical notes do not create images in our mind. It is important to remember that when we are doing any work, our brain is already generating one set of pictures. When we listen to a song, another set of pictures is generated. We see the actors and actresses dancing together, the background scene etc. Nature has created us in such a way that our brain at one point of time can create only one set of pictures. Thus, when we listen to songs **that have words** (and which trigger a set of images) our concentration is greatly affected.

'Do not listen to the walkman while studying.'

Remember, focus or concentration produces results. It allows us to direct our energy and attention to the attainment of a specific goal.

2. SPEED MATHEMATICS

Mathematics is one of the most important subjects taught in schools and colleges. In western countries, students are introduced to the calculator at an early age. The calculator can be used for arithmetic but what about Algebra? Anyway, it is always useful to be able to calculate fast.

There are many books which teach various methods of rapid calculation. These methods are easy to understand. Also these methods have unity, i.e., many techniques are similar. No author can claim any copyright for any techniques of speed calculation, simply because mathematics is not the invention of this generation.

I have given here many simple and useful techniques for multiplication, and for calculating squares, square roots and cube roots. These are written for students of average intelligence level.

SPEED MULTIPLICATION

Multiplication of a single digit number by a single digit number is child's play. However, to multiply a two-digit by a two-digit or a three-digit number requires some effort. Here, I have described methods of multiplying two, three and four digit numbers. The same technique can be expanded for numbers of higher digits.

Multiplying a two digit number by a two digit number

The traditional method:

```
        23              67
     x  12           x  32
     ------          ------
        46             134
    + 230           + 2010
     ------          ------
       276            2144
```

By speed calculation

Step 1

$$2 \qquad 3$$
$$\downarrow$$
$$1 \qquad 2$$
$$\overline{\qquad}$$
$$6$$

We multiply the digits in the ones place, that is, 3 x 2 = 6. We write 6 in the ones place of the answer.

Step 2

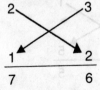

Now, we cross multiply and add the products, that is, (2 x 2) + (1 x 3) = 7. We write the 7 in the tens place of the answer.

Step 3

$$2 \qquad 3$$
$$\downarrow$$
$$1 \qquad 2$$
$$\overline{\qquad}$$
$$2 \quad 7 \quad 6$$

Now we multiply the digits on the extreme left that is, 2 x 1 = 2.

The completed multiplication is:

$$
\begin{array}{r}
23 \\
\times \ 12 \\
\hline
276
\end{array}
$$

An average 10 to 12-year child can solve this problem in less than 8 seconds. Well, so you see for yourself how effective speed mathematics is in saving you time and labour. Also, it makes arithmetic more interesting. Many of my friends never liked calculations. But when I started teaching them speed mathematics they began to enjoy it. I often made them compete against themselves to induce the fighting spirit. They started calculating so fast that they could beat their parents.

Let us have a look at another simple example. Let us take 31 multiplied by 25

Step 1

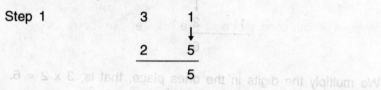

```
      3       1
              ↓
      2       5
      _____
              5
```

Step 2

```
      3       1
        ✕
      2       5
      _____
      7       5
```

Cross multiplication gives us a two-digit answer: (3 x 5) + (2 x 1) = 17. Write 7 in the tens place of the answer and carry over 1.

STEP 3

```
      3       1
      ↓
      2       5
      _____
  7   7       5
```

Remember to add the carried over number to the product of the ones digits here: (3 x 2) + 1 = 7

In the above examples we multiplied a two-digit number by a two-digit number. Now we go on to multiply a three-digit number by a three-digit number.

STEP 1

```
  *   *   *       1   2   1
                          ↓
  *   *   *       3   4   5
  _____
                          5
```

Multiply the digits in the ones place of both the numbers.

STEP 2

```
  *       *   *       1   2   1
            ✕
  *       *   *       3   4   5
  _____
                      4   5
```

14

Cross multiply the ones and tens digits:

(2 x 5) + (4 x 1) = 14.

Write 4 in the tens place of the answer and carry over 1.

STEP 3

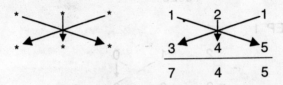

Multiply the digits in the tens place and cross multiply the digits in the hundreds and ones places, and add the products and the carried over number: (1 x 5) + (2 x 4) + (3 x 1) + 1 = 17. Write 7 in the hundreds place of the answer and carry over 1.

STEP 4

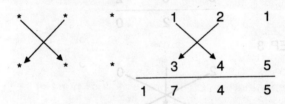

Cross-multiply the digits in the tens and hundreds places, and add the product and the number carried over: (1 x 4) + (3 x 2) + 1 = 11. Write 1 in the thousands place of the answer and carry over 1.

STEP 5

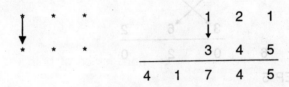

Multiply the digits in the hundreds place in the two numbers, and add the number carried over: (1 x 3) + 1 = 4

15

Let us take the example of multiplication of two three-digit numbers.

$$
\begin{array}{r}
210 \\
\times\ 362 \\
\hline
76020
\end{array}
$$

STEP 1

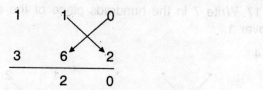

```
    2    1    0
              ↓
  x 3    6    2

              0
```

STEP 2

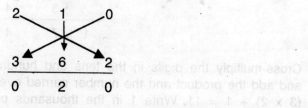

```
  1    1    0
  3    6    2
  ─────────
       2    0
```

STEP 3

```
  2    1    0
  3    6    2
  0    2    0
```

STEP 4

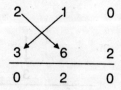

```
  2    1    0
  3    6    2
6 0    2    0
```

STEP 5

```
     2    1    0
     ↓
     3    6    2
7 6  0    2    0
```

16

If we want to multiply a two-digit number by a three-digit number, we simply add a zero in the hundreds place of the two-digit number to make it a three-digit number. The same method gives us the correct answer.

For example, if you want to multiply 175 by 89, write the multiplication problem as:

$$
\begin{array}{ccc}
1 & 7 & 5 \\
\times\,0 & 8 & 9 \\
\hline
\end{array}
$$

We can extend the logic of multiplication of two three-digit numbers, to multiplication of two **four-digit numbers**. I have shown below the method extended for four-digit numbers. You can extend the technique for five-digit, six-digit and higher numbers.

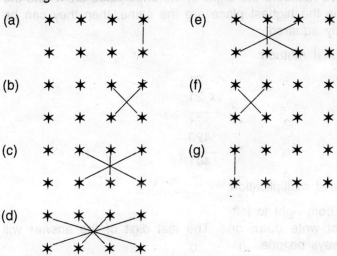

When we multiplied two-digit numbers, we used 3 steps. When we multiplied three-digit numbers, we used 5 steps. When we multiplied four-digit numbers , we used 7 steps. The formula to find out the number of steps is: $(2 \times n) - 1$ where n is the number of digits in the number to be multiplied.

For a two-digit number $(2 \times 2) - 1 = 3$

For a three-digit number $(2 \times 3) - 1 = 5$
For a four-digit number $(2 \times 4) - 1 = 7$

Also, the first and the last steps are mirror images of each other, the second and the second last steps are mirror images of each other, the third and the third last step are mirror images of each other and so on......

INSTANT SQAURING

Method 1

Suppose you want to calculate what is the square of 21 without using your calculator. You can use this technique that says

'If in two numbers the digits in the ones place are 1 and the digits in the highest place are the same, then they can be instantly squared.'

Traditional method:

$$\begin{array}{r} 21 \\ \times\ 21 \\ \hline 21 \\ 420 \\ \hline 441 \end{array}$$

By speed multiplication:

Begin from right to left
- Just write down one. The last digit of the answer will always be one
- $2 + 2 = 4$ (Answer = _41)
- $2 \times 2 = 4$ (Answer = 441)

$$\begin{array}{r} 31 \\ \times\ 31 \\ \hline 961 \end{array}$$

- Write down 1
- $3 + 3 = 6$
- $3 \times 3 = 9$

18

Suppose you want to multiply 101 by 101

$$101$$
$$\times\ 101$$
$$10201$$

- Write down 1 as usual. 1 multiplied by 1 is 1. The remaining set of numbers is 10.
- 10 + 10 = 20. Write down 0 and carry over 2
- 10 x 10 = 100 plus 2 carried over is 102. So, the answer is 10201.

Method 2

In Method 1, we had the digits in the ones place adding up to 2. Method 2 is used when the digits in the ones place add up to 10 and the remaining digits are the same. Let us have a look at some examples.

$$35$$
$$\times\ 35$$
$$12\ 25$$

- In the ones place, 5 x 5 = 25.
- In the tens place we multiply the digit by the number that follows it, i.e., (3 + 1) = 4 giving 3 x 4 = 12.

$$45$$
$$45$$
$$20\ 25$$

- 5 x 5 = 25
- 4 x 5 = 20)

$$125$$
$$125$$
$$156/25$$
$$15625$$

19

- 5 x 5 = 25
- 12 x 13 = 156

Let us have a look at other examples:

$$
\begin{array}{r}
64 \\
\times\ 66 \\
\hline
42/24 \\
\hline
4224 \\
\end{array}
$$

Here the extreme most digits total up to 10. Also, the remaining digits are the same (both are 6) So, the second law is applicable.

$$
\begin{array}{r}
31 \\
\times\ 39 \\
\hline
12/09 \\
\hline
1209 \\
\end{array}
$$ (1 x 9 = 9, but as a rule we always write down 09)

Method 3

Method 3 is used to square all the numbers that lie between 50 and 60.

(a)
$$
\begin{array}{r}
53 \\
\times\ 53 \\
\hline
28/09 \\
\end{array}
$$

- We start from right to left. Three squared is 9, so we write down 9. But the product of the digits in the ones place should give a two-digit number. We convert 9 into a two-digit number and write down 09.

- We square the digit in the tens place and add to the result the digit in the ones place: (5 x 5) + 3 = 28.

(b)
$$
\begin{array}{r}
57 \\
\times\ 57 \\
\hline
3249 \\
\end{array}
$$

The digit in the ones place, 7, squared gives us 49. The digit in the tens place gives us (5 x 5) + 7 = 32.

(c)   59
                                        x 59
                                        ____
                                        3481

INSTANT SQUARE ROOTS

The system of finding square roots that I have explained in the book is only for perfect squares. This technique will not enable you to find imperfect square roots. However, in most competitive and school examinations only perfect squares are asked.

BASIC REQUIREMENTS

If the square ends in	the square root ends in
1	9 or 1
4	8 or 2
5	5
6	6 or 4
9	7 or 3
0	0

We see that if the square ends in 1, the square root ends in 1 or 9. If the square ends in 4, the square root ends either in 8 or in 2 and so on...
No perfect square ends in 2, 3, 7, or 8.

Standard squares for reference:
$10^2 = 100$
$20^2 = 400$
$30^2 = 900$
$40^2 = 1600$
$50^2 = 2500$
$60^2 = 3600$
$70^2 = 4900$
$80^2 = 6400$
$90^2 = 8100$
$100^2 = 10000$

Suppose we want to find the square root of 5184.

- 5184 ends in 4. So the square root ends in either 2 or 8 (Answer = __2 or __8).

- 5184 is between 4900 (70²) and 6400 (80²). So the square root is between 70 and 80. The two possibilities are 72 and 78.

- Out of 4900 and 6400, our number 5184 is more close to 4900 than to 6400. Out of the two possibilities 72 and 78, 72 is more close to 70. Thus, the correct answer is 72.

Let us find the square root of 529.

- 529 ends in 9. So, the square root ends either in 3 or in 7.
- 529 is between is 400 (20²) and 900 (30²). So, the square root is either 23 or 27.
- 529 is more close to 400. Out of 23 and 27, 23 is more close to 20. Thus, the correct answer is 23.

Let us find the square root of 2304.

- 2304 ends in 4 and so the root ends in either 2 or 8.
- 2304 lies between 1600 and 2500. So, the root lies between 40 and 50.
- Thus, the two possibilities are 42 and 48.
- Also, 2304 is more close to 2500 (50 x 50). Thus, out of 42 and 48, 48 is more close to 50 and so 48 is the answer.

We have seen a system of instant square rooting. I have limited myself to the square roots which are less than 100 because only such numbers are included in competitive examinations. However, the same technique can be further expanded.

CUBE ROOTS

The techniques of finding square roots and cube roots that I have described are only for perfect squares and cubes.

We saw that we can find the square root by observing the

last digit of the number given. However, there were two possibilities. For example, if the number ended with a 4, the square root would either end in 8 or 2. If the number ended in 6, the square root would end either in 4 or 6 and so on. But while deriving the cube root, the possibility is always for one number.

number	cube	last digit of cube	last digit of cube root
1	1	1	1
2	8	8	2
3	27	7	3
4	64	4	4
5	125	5	5
6	216	6	6
7	343	3	7
8	512	2	8
9	729	9	9
10	1000	0	0

You can see that if the last digit of the cube or the cube root is 0, 1, 4, 5, 6 or 9, the cube root or cube respectively, ends in the same digit. There are pairs 2 and 8, and 3 and 7 such that if the cube or the cube root ends in one of these numbers, the cube root or the cube respectively, ends in the other.

Whenever you are given a number and are asked to find the cube root, make a box around the last three digits and underline the remaining digits.

Suppose the number given to you is 117649 and you are asked to find the cube root. You take the last three digits, namely 649 and put a box around it. You take the remaining digits and underline them.

Thus, 117649 will be written

<u>117</u> | 649 |

Suppose you are given 10648. Write it as

Thus, 10648 becomes, <u>10</u> | 648 |

Find the cube root of <u>103</u> $\boxed{823}$

As, the given number ends with a 3, the cube root ends with a 7.

Answer at this stage is __7.

Now, look at the other digits (103). Take the number formed by the underlined digits. Find the cubes nearest this number. The cubes are 64 (cube of 4) and 125 (cube of 5). When represented on a number line, 103 lies between 64 and 125. Now, as a rule we always take the lower number. I repeat. It is a rule and so we always follow it. We take the lower number of 64 and 125. The smaller/lower number is 64 (which is the cube of 4). The previous answer we got was __7. Now fill in the number 4 in the blank space.

Thus, 47 is the cube root of 103823.

Find the cube root of <u>262</u> $\boxed{144}$

Since, 262144 ends with a 4, the cube root ends with a 4. The answer at this stage is (__4). Also, 262 is between 216 (the cube of 6) and 343 (the cube of 7). Out of 216 and 343, we take the lower number that is 216. The cube root of 216 is 6. The previous answer that we got was __4. Now, we fill in the 6 in the blank part. The final answer is 64.

Find the cube root of <u>12</u> $\boxed{167}$

Since, the cube root ends with a 7, the root ends with a 3. Answer at this stage is __3. The underlined part of the number is 12, which lies between 8 (the cube of 2) and 27 (the cube of 3). As a rule we take the lower number of 8. The cube root of 8 is 2. Thus, the final answer is 23.

The Base Method of Multiplication

The base method of multiplication is very different from the other methods of multiplication. Whenever I give demonstrations on stage and ask people to give me two digit, three digit, four digit numbers to multiply mentally, they usually come up with big numbers like 99, 997, 9989, 99999 etc. They think that the bigger the number, the more difficult it will be for me to calculate. It will be tedious, and I will be more likely to make a mistake. But the truth is exactly the opposite, the higher the number of 9's and 8's, the easier it is for me to calculate. It only makes my work simpler.

This method is called the base method, because here we take certain bases that are always in the powers of 10 such as 10, 100, 1000, 10000 etc. Whenever we are asked to find the square of a number or asked to multiply two numbers, we select an appropriate base.

If we are asked to find the square of 97, then we will take the base of 100 rather than taking the base of 10 as 97 is closer to 100. If we are asked to multiply 997 by 984, we will take the base of 1000 as both 997 and 984 are close to 1000.

Suppose we are asked to multiply 89 by 99. We take the base as 100 and write down as follows:

$$89 - 11$$
$$99 - 1$$

- First we write down 89 from the question.
- Since 89 is **less** than 100, we put a **minus** sign.
- The difference between 89 and 100 is 11 and so we write down 11.
- Similarly for the other number 99.

Thus, when we multiply 987 by 993, we will write it as (taking the base as 1000),

$$987 - 13 \quad (987 \text{ is } 1000 \text{ minus } 13)$$
$$993 - 7 \quad (993 \text{ is } 1000 \text{ minus } 7)$$

To find the square of 99999, we will write, (Taking base as 100000)

$$99999 - 1$$
$$99999 - 1$$

Now, this was the writing part. It is very simple. And the solving is still simpler. The solving involves two steps.

The first step involves multiplying the numbers to the right of the minus sign. '*But the number of digits in the product*

*thus obtained should be equal to the number of zeros in
the base.'*

(A)	(B)	(C)
89 - 11	987 - 13	99999 - 1
99 - 1	993 - 7	99999 - 1
11	091	00001

In (A), the base is 100, which has **two zeros**, thus the
product of 11 into 1 is written as 11, which is also a **two
digit** answer. So, the number of digits is equal to the number of zeros.

In (B), the base is 1000, which has 3 zeros. So, the product
13 x 7 which is 91 is written as 091.

In (C), the base is 100000, which has 5 zeros. So, the
product of 1 into 1 is written as 00001.

Thus we have obtained one part of the answer. The other
part is obtained by cross-subtracting.

(A)	(B)	(C)
89 - 11	987 - 13	99999 - 1
99 - 1	993 - 7	99999 - 1
88/11	**980**/091	**99998**/00001

In (A), 88 is obtained by cross-subtracting 89 minus 1 OR
99 minus 11.

In (B), 980 is obtained by cross-subtracting 987 minus 7
OR 993 minus 13.

In (C), 99998 is obtained by cross-subtracting 99999 minus
1 OR 99999 minus 1.

Whichever cross-subtraction we take, the answer is always
the same. Thus, we can take any cross-subtraction that we
find easy. In example (A), 89 minus 1 is relatively easier
than 99 minus 11.

Another example:

Let us multiply 850 by 994. Taking as the base 1000, which has 3 zeros.

$$
\begin{array}{r}
850 - 150 \\
994 - 6 \\
\hline
844\ /\ 900
\end{array}
$$

- We multiply 150 by 6 and get the answer as 900. It is a three digit number equal to the number of zeros in 1000.

- We take the cross subtraction of 850 minus 6 as 844 and write down the answer.

In this part we saw how to multiply digits like 99, 986, 8997 etc. which are less than their bases of 100, 1000, 10000. But suppose we have numbers like 12, 110, 1099, 10076 which are above their bases. For that too we can use the same method but instead of subtracting we will use addition. Let us have a look at three examples with different bases.

(A) Multiply 12 by 13 (The base is 10)

$$
\begin{array}{r}
12 + 2 \\
13 + 3 \\
\hline
\mathbf{15\ /\ 6}
\end{array}
$$

- Since 12 is 2 over the base 10, we write 12 as 12 + 2. Similarly, 13.

- Multiply 2 by 3 in the right hand part. The answer is 6 which is a one-digit answer. (The number of zero's in 10 is also 1.)

- Now, take the cross addition of 12 plus 3 or 13 plus 2 and the answer is 15.

(B) Multiply 1072 by 1003 (The base is 1000)

$$
\begin{array}{r}
1072 + 72 \\
1003 + 03 \\
\hline
\mathbf{1075\ /\ 216}
\end{array}
$$

27

- We multiply the right hand parts i.e. 72 into 3 and write the answer as 216

- We take the cross addition of 1072 and 3, which is 1075.

(C) We multiply 10093 by 10003 using base as 10000

$$10093 + 93$$
$$10003 + 03$$
$$\overline{10096 \,/\, 0279}$$

- 93 into 3 is 279
- 1093 plus 3 is 1096.

Thus, we saw the base method of multiplication wherein digits are close to a base. Either both the numbers in the question are less than the base or both the numbers more than the base.

What do you do when the product of the right hand part of the answer exceeds the number of 0s in the base? If the base is 100 which has two zeros and the right hand part of the answer is a three-digit number, then we have to use an additional step. Carry over the highest place digit in the right part of the number to the left part.

Let us take a few examples.

When 112 is multiplied by 110 (base is 100 with two zeros)

$$112 + 12$$
$$110 + 10$$
$$\overline{122 \,/\, 120}$$

According to our normal base method of multiplying, the answer of the right hand part is 12 x 10 = 120. And the left hand part is 112 plus 10 which is 122. This gives 122120.

But, 120 is a three-digit number and the number of zeros in 100 is two. Thus, our answer 122120 is not the correct answer. In this situation, in order to get a correct answer we add the numbers which are immediately to the left and right of the stroke.

$$1 \quad 2 \boxed{2 / 1} \quad 2 \quad 0$$

Thus, in order to get the answer we add 2 plus 1 which is 3.

The answer is 12320.

(D) Multiply 1200 by 1020. (The base 1000 has three zeros.)

$$
\begin{array}{r}
1200 + 200 \\
1020 + 20 \\
\hline
1220 \,/\, 4000
\end{array}
$$

The normal system gives us the answer of 12204000. Add the numbers immediately to the left and right of the slash: $0 + 4 = 4$.

$$1 \quad 2 \quad 2 \quad \mathbf{0 + 4} \quad 0 \quad 0 \quad 0$$

The final answer is 1224000

Multiply 131 by 112. (The base is 100 which has two zeros.)

$$
\begin{array}{r}
131 + 31 \\
112 + 12 \\
\hline
143 \,/\, 372 \\
\text{gives} \ 14672
\end{array}
$$

In the above example, we got $3 + 3 = 6$. So, we wrote down 6. In some examples, we have to add $6 + 6$ instead of $3 + 3$. But, $6 + 6$ will give us 12 which is a two-digit number and again we will have to write down 2 and carry over 1 to the digit on the left. Two examples of this follow.

Multiply 18 by 17.

$$
\begin{array}{r}
18 + 8 \\
17 + 7 \\
\hline
25 \,/\, 56
\end{array}
$$

29

We begin solving the answer from right to left.

First, we write down 6 as it is

_____6

Then, since the right hand part 56 has more digits than the number of zeros in the base 10, we add the digit immediately to the left and right of the slash: 5 + 5 = 10. Here, we write down a 0 and carry over 1.

_____06

Add the one that is carried over to the 2 in 25 to the left of the slash: 2 + 1 = 3.

Final answer: 306

Multiply 19 by 18

$$19 + 9$$
$$18 + 8$$

$$27 / 72$$

The base 10 has one zero and 72 has two digits. So, again we need to carry over.

We add the digits immediately to the left and right of the slash. 7 plus 7 is 14. So, we write down 4 and carry over 1. Add the one that is carried over to the left.

Final Answer: 342

You can use the base method to multiply two numbers one above and the other below the base.

Multiply 171 by 99. (The base is 100.)

$$171 + 71$$
$$99 - 01$$

We have two opposite signs and there are ways to find the answer. But, in such cases the base method proves time consuming. We can use other ways of multiplying.

This was the base method of multiplication. We have taken numbers such as 10, 100, 1000 etc. as bases. There are

30

similar techniques which let you take bases like 50, 40, 60 etc.

I have taught you two methods of multiplication. You have already learnt one method in school. Thus, you have three methods with you. Whenever, you take up a question, decide which method will be the most appropriate and then proceed accordingly. If you are asked to multiply 99 by 99, you may prefer the base method, as the numbers are close to the base 100. But if you are asked to multiply 23 by 79, then the base method will prove ineffective and you can use your normal way of multiplying. The important thing is get well versed with all the methods of multiplication. Many people argue with me what is the use of learning all this when we all have the calculator and computer with us. But, 'Nothing that is learnt in life is useless.'

In the beginning of the section, I had told you that speed mathematics can help you immensely in competitive examinations. Here are a few exercises for practice.

1. Which of these is the square root of 1024?

    [A] 33   [B] 32   [C] 34   [D] 35

2. Which of these is the root of 2704?

    [A] 82   [B] 88   [C] 52   [D] 48

3. Which of these is the correct product of 314 and 546?

    [A] 171444 [B] 171454 [C] 171534 [D] 171554

4. Which of these is the cube root of 17576?

    [A] 28   [B] 26   [C] 24   [D] 32

5. Which is the cube root of 175616

    [A] 46   [B] 56   [C] 66   [D] 76

6. What is 93 multiplied by 94?

    [A] 8742   [B] 8472   [C] 8442   [D] 8772

Answers and explanations

1. The number 1024 ends with a 4. So, obviously the root should end with a 2 or an 8. Among the alternatives

given, 32 is the only possibility as no other alternative ends in 2 or 8. Hence, 32 is the answer.

2. Because 2704 lies between 2500 (the square of 50) and 3600 (the square of 60), the root should lie between 50 and 60. Hence the correct answer is 52.

3. Using speed multiplication, as soon as you get the last two digit of the answer, namely 44 you know that the correct answer is alternative A. This happens because in speed multiplication, there are no intermediate steps involved in multiplication. The number you build is the final answer. You build it from the right, that is, from the ones place. After the first step, your answer is __4. After the second step, your answer is __44. You get your answer at this stage as alternative A. You need not complete the multiplication.

4. Since the number ends in 6, the root has to end in 6. No other given alternative ends in 6. So, the answer is 26.

5. Since the number 175616 lies the between the cube of 50 which is 125000 and 60 which is 216000, the cube root of 175616 lies between 50 and 60. The last digit of the number is 6, and therefore the last digit of the cube root is 6. The correct answer is 56.

6. Using the base method of multiplication, we instantly get the correct answer as A.

3. TIME MANAGEMENT

Consider any two individuals. They go to school, play, chat with friends, surf the net, watch TV etc. But they get different results in the examinations. Sometimes, their results have a big difference.

There can be many reasons why one individual performs better than another. One of the reasons is the difference in time management. One person correctly prioritises things in order of their importance while the other just drifts along doing things at random. One individual has a fixed target in mind while the other does not.

In this chapter, we will discuss the importance of time management. If time management is instilled in childhood, it will become a lifelong habit. Therefore, time management should be taken seriously.

We are but minutes, little things,

Each one furnished with sixty wings
With which we fly on our unseen track
And not one of us ever comes back.

We are but minutes use us well,
For how we are used, we must some day tell,
Who uses minutes has hours to use,
Who loses minutes –whole years must lose
— Anonymous

Stephen Covey has written many international bestsellers. His most widely read book is *The Seven Habits of Highly Effective People*. Stephen Covey has given various tips and suggestions to cultivate these habit in our lives. The second and the third habit deal with time management. Covey says that we must learn to prioritise things. 'Put first things first.' Some things are important, some things are urgent. How we prioritise amongst these urgent and important assignments is time management. There are four combinations of these

- Urgent and important work
- Urgent but not important work
- Important but not urgent work
- Not important and not urgent work

We must give first priority to the work that is urgent as well as important. It **must be done**. Then, comes that work which is urgent but which is not important. Since, it is urgent, again it has to be done. After that, comes that work which is important to be completed but not urgent. And the fact that it is not urgent, gives it less preference to the work that is urgent. And finally comes that work which is neither important nor urgent. It is the last priority.

We must divide our activities into these four groups and learn to give them priority accordingly.

Also, we must have a definite plan of how we will go about doing things. Covey says that in order to solve any jigsaw puzzle we need two things

- The small pieces that will help us to solve the puzzle.
- A solution picture at which we can look and solve the puzzle.

Covey says, 'Begin with the end in mind.' Have a goal in mind before doing anything. Before you prioritise the small minutes and hours at your disposal, you must have a target that you want to set for yourself. Suppose you are doing a jigsaw puzzle. How will you do it? Unless you have something to look at (the solution picture) how will you arrange the pieces? Similarly, your goal is like a picture and the time at your disposal is like the jigsaw pieces. In order to manage time, we must have a definite goal in mind. Plan your activities according to your requirements. So, the first law of efficient time management is 'Prioritise your needs', on the basis of their urgency and importance.

The second law of time-management is to **'Be consistent'**.

There was a boy called Mike who loved basketball. Every

day he used to play basketball for hours and hours together. One day, his mother asked him, "Son, you will be appearing for your exams soon. Why don't you study?"

Mike replied, "Mom, you know that I can easily study a day before the examination and get good marks. So, why should I study now?" His mom did not say anything and Mike went away to play. When he returned home he said, "Mummy, Can you please make a cake for me to-morrow? You know how much I like it."

The next day when Mike asked his Mother about the cake, his mother said, "Sorry, son. But I forgot to make it. I will definitely make it to-morrow." This went on for three days. On the fourth day, Mike's mom made him the cake. "I want a big one, a really big piece of cake. After all, I want to eat three days' cake in a day." said Mike. So, he got three big pieces of creamy chocolate cake. But he found he could not eat it.

His mom said, "This is exactly what I wanted to teach you. You cannot eat three days' cake at once and similarly you cannot do a month's work in a day."

Mike's mother was right. We cannot think of studying the whole book on the eve of the examination. Continuous practice is a must. Regularity is the key word. You will soon learn about a powerful technique called frequent revision technique (FRT) later. The reason why FRT is so useful is because it demands regular revision from the student.

'Time is a circus always packing up and moving away.'
— Ben Hecht

Jason never studied until the day before the examination. This was his habit. When the results were announced, he used to get average marks. A day before his Standard IX examinations, his father had an accident and was hospitalised. Jason spent the night at his father's bedside. Though he wrote his examination, he failed.

'Time goes, you say? Ah no!
Alas, time stays, we go.
— Austin Dobson

Whenever you are setting a time frame for yourself, take into consideration your past. I know of a student who made a timetable for starting his studies on a particular day. But that day never came. Another would decide that the next whole week he would study for eight hours a day. But he had never done so much work in a day. He found he could not study for more than three hours a day.

Whenever you are planning a timetable, take into consideration your habits and stamina. Ask yourself honestly how much work you can do and how much work you have done before.

The second virtue needed for efficient time-management is Be consistent and give sincere efforts.

The third quality required is the art of Living in the present.

'The right moment to do anything is now. This moment is the golden moment, use it.'

The third quality is 'focus on the present.' Many of us have a habit of dreaming about the future and feeling sad about the past. We want to live in the future and the past but not in the present. This daydreaming becomes a part of our thinking. Sometimes, for a long span of time, we keep on thinking about our bright future (no one thinks about a dull future) just to suddenly realise that we are not in our dreamland but here in the present. Someone has said,

"The past is history; the future is a mystery. The present is a gift and so it is called THE PRESENT."

Many people worry about the future. Worry never helped anybody. In fact, it is said, 'There are only two things to worry about in the future. Either you can change a thing or else you cannot change it. Well, if you can change it, there is nothing to worry about because at the right time you will be able to change it. Also, if you are not able to change it, you do not have to worry because in any case worrying will not enable you to change it!'

You must use the present to plan your future. Once you

prioritise your activities on the basis of their urgency and importance, you have a list of things for which you must spare time. Now, you have to decide how much time you are going to allot for each of them.

This is the time for 'down-to-earth' thinking. When I had just entered my teens, I would decide that I would not watch TV or read storybooks until the examinations. But somehow, I was never able to control my desire to watch my favourite shows on TV or read fewer books. My father advised me to take into consideration my past habits. He was the first person to teach me 'down-to-earth' thinking and time management.

From then on, whenever I set a time frame for myself, I used to allow time for reading books, watching TV, chatting with friends, etc. All this helped me a lot.

So, the important thing is to focus on the present. Accept your habits and interests which you cannot change suddenly. Take these into account whenever you set a time frame for work.

Some of your habits will be positive. Reading self-improvement books and watching worthy shows on television is good for you. You can always spare time for these activities. But, some of your habits can be harmful. You may be addicted to these. Instead of refreshing and rejuvenating you, they will waste a lot of your time. You can use your subconscious mind to get rid of them. (Refer to chapter 9 for Sub-Conscious study.) Your love and attachment towards your negative habits will be gradually reduced by your subconscious mind.

So, the third law of effective time management is, don't lose yourself in the past and don't dream of the future. Focus on the present because it is a gift.

> Sure there is lots of trouble
> Sure there are heaps of cares,
> Burdens that bend us double,
> Worries that come to wear.
> But we must keep pursuing

Something, and see it through;
Still to be up and doing
All that there is to do.
Though you would like to idle,
Wait for the world to be right,
Keep your hand on the bridle,
Fight when you have to fight.
Women are won by wooing
Fortune is won the same,
And to be up and doing
Is all there is to the game.
Few ever fail by trying
Few ever win who wait
All of your sitting and sighing
Never will conquer fate.
Whatever path you're hewing,
One thing is certain, son;
Either be up and doing
Or you'll be down and done.

— Douglas Malloch.

And the most important requirement to efficiently manage
time is to stop procrastinating.

The clock of life is wound but once
And no man has the power
To tell just when the hands will stop
At late or early hour.
Now is the only time you own
Live, love, work with a will,
Place no faith in tomorrow,
For the clock may then be still.

Don't procrastinate. Procrastination means postponing deci-
sions. We have a set of things to do today and we decide
that we will do them tomorrow, and tomorrow we may decide to do them the day after tomorrow. We postpone until
the last moment and do a job only when it is very urgent.

Can any country afford to train its soldiers at the last moment? Can a military general say, "If we train soldiers but

38

there is no war, all the money and effort will be wasted." A country has to be ready to face any challenge and at any time. Many people are like this military general. They never do their work till the last moment. But the last moment is never the best time to do any work. You cannot achieve your best when you are under pressure, even in a panic.

'I recommend you to take care of the minutes, for the hours will take care of themselves.'

— Chesterfield

Joe never completed his science journal on time. He was always late for submission. One day before his practical examinations he would plead with his friend to help him with the experiments. At the last moment, he would draw haphazard diagrams and write untidy experiments. No wonder, he always did badly.

Time once lost cannot be got back. We do not have a time machine. Time passes in a one-way direction. So stop procrastinating and act right now, for the right moment to do anything is this.

'God made time, but man made haste.'

— Irish Proverb

I wrote the first page of this book many months ago when I was in 11th standard. I had a definite plan in mind about this book. I had a fixed target in mind to finish it before a certain date because the next year would be crucial in my life. But, I did not take my work seriously. I never made this book my first priority. I kept on postponing it. Sometimes, I wanted to play cricket or TV games etc. I wanted to do anything but write my book. The year passed and I had managed to write very little. During 12th standard, I did not join any coaching classes for the experience of studying on my own. Days passed by and I did not realise the importance of time. My deadline for the book was approaching. I wanted the best student of the year award that would be announced in January. My annual examinations were scheduled for February. There was only a month's gap between the two!

The fact is that I did manage to complete the book on time and got the award. But, only at the cost of a much poor performance than was possible. I postponed my work and so I had to face the consequences. It was a tough lesson that life taught me.

If you have work to do,
Do it now
Today the skies are clear and blue
Tomorrow clouds may come in view
Yesterday is not for you
Do it now.

C. Northcote Parkinson gave a wonderful law: Work expands so as to fill the time available for its completion.

The law explains that work will take the time that you decide to spend on it. Let me give you an example. Suppose I am studying financial management and I decide to solve 30 problems in 5 hours. Then, I will only solve them in 5 hours and not in less time. I may take up more time, but the general tendency is that we will never be able to finish it in a shorter time period. If I decide to solve the sums in 7 hours then I will only be able to solve those 30 sums in 7 hours. If I decide to spend 8 hours, then somehow I will end up finishing the sums only in 8 hours. If we allocate more time than necessary, then somehow we become lazy and lethargic and manage to finish that job only in that time.

That is precisely the reason why managers in companies give the bare minimum time to their staff to finish any work. They know that if they give more time or a flexible deadline, the staff will finish the job only at the last moment. Thus, they give minimum time to employees to finish their work. When you plan your schedule, you should allocate reasonably sufficient time for yourself to finish the work.

◫

4. NRT / FRT

Now, we take up a method of study that is helpful in the long run. All the other techniques which are mentioned in this book are specific to a particular purpose. FRT is different in the sense it applies to any work. It is based on the principle that consistency is the key to success.

In order to understand both the methods of studying - NRT and FRT — we will take the example of a student in each case and observe his studying pattern for a time period. Then we will comparatively evaluate our conclusions thus obtained.

The intention of this chapter is to make the reader understand how we forget what we have learnt as time passes by. The two factors involved are memory level (ML) that will be shown on the y-axis and time that will be shown on the x-axis of the graphs. To make our study easier, we will assume that it takes an effort of one hour to push the memory level to 20 per cent and so it will take five hours to push the memory level to 100 per cent.

The first technique is:

Normal Revision Technique

NRT is followed by most of the students most of the time. The pattern here is: 'we study and as time passes by, we forget and so we study again and again.'

We take the example of Mark who is a student in Grade 9. He has decided to study history during the month of December. Mark is a very good student. His favourite subjects are mathematics, English, Physics and Spanish. The problem with him is that he forgets theoretical subjects like history, geography very easily. He scores exceptionally good marks in mathematics, sciences, and languages. Because of the other subjects, his average score is lower.

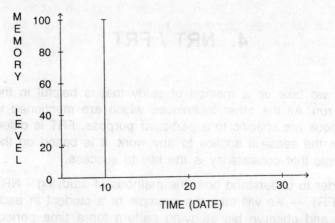

TIME (DATE)

In the above graph we have taken time on the X-axis and the memory level of the individual on the Y-axis. We will measure memory level in percentages. Throughout we will assume that it takes one hour to take your memory level to 20 per cent and so it will take five hours to take your memory level to 100 per cent.

The date is 10th of December. Mark gets up early in the morning and opens his history textbook. He studies for around five hours. (We have assumed that in five hours you reach 100 per cent memory.) After studying for five hours, he is convinced that he knows everything. His father gives him a test and is happy to see that his son has done so well.

Now, as time passes by, Mark gradually forgets what he has learnt. So, the graph looks like this.

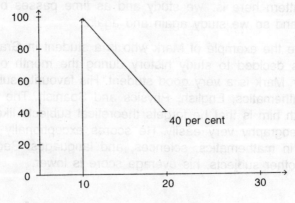

40 per cent

Now, the date is 20th December. From the graph it can be seen that Mark has forgotten 60 per cent of what he had studied, and remembers 40 per cent. Have a look at point A on the graph.

So, he decides to work hard for **three hours** and push his memory level back to 100 per cent.

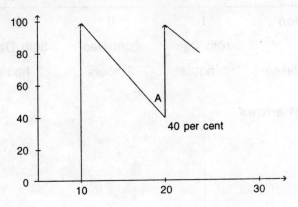

Further, as time passes by, his memory level keeps dropping.

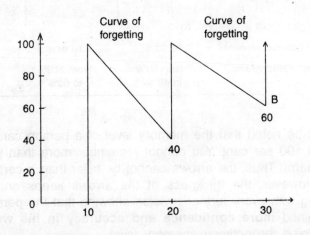

Point B on 30th December indicates that Mark remembers only 60 per cent of the subject matter. Thus, he decides to study history for the third time and after working hard for two hours, he is able to push his memory level back to 100 per cent.

On 31st December he writes the examination.

OBSERVATION CHART

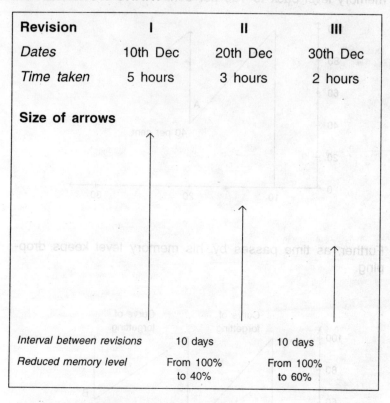

Revision	I	II	III
Dates	10th Dec	20th Dec	30th Dec
Time taken	5 hours	3 hours	2 hours

Size of arrows

Interval between revisions	10 days	10 days
Reduced memory level	From 100% to 40%	From 100% to 60%

It must be noted that the memory level of a person cannot exceed 100 per cent. You cannot remember more than you have learnt. Thus, the arrows cannot be taller than a certain limit. However, the thickness of the arrows keeps on increasing with every further revision showing that the person has gained **more confidence and accuracy in his work** maintaining the optimum memory level.

Also it should be noted that the amount of hard work in terms of time such as five hours a day, three hours a day is used only by way of an example. At lower levels of education there is hardly anyone who puts in *so much effort every day.* So, do not be frightened when I speak of five hours a day or four hours a day etc.

Thus, we observe in NRT that as time passes by, a student forgets his subject matter and so he has to study again. Now, we will observe FRT.

Frequent Revision Technique (FRT)

'Consistency' is the principle on which the system of FRT is based.

Nicky had decided to study history on 10th December. After working hard for five hours, he asked his mother to test him. His mother was happy to see that he knew everything so well.

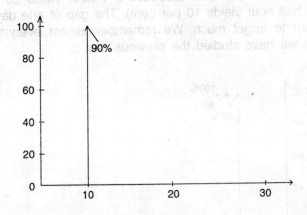

She patted him on his back and went inside the kitchen to make some ice cream for him. Nicky ate the ice cream and went to sleep. While he slept, he forgot 10 per cent of what he had learnt and his memory level dropped to 90 per cent.

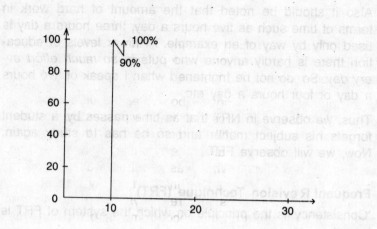

Next day when he got up in the morning, Nicky studied history again. Since, he remembered most of what he had learnt the previous day, it took him only half an hour to recollect everything and push his ML (memory level) from 90 per cent to 100 per cent (because if 1 hour yields 20 per cent; a half hour yields 10 per cent). The gap of one day is too short to forget much. We remember almost everything of what we have studied the previous day.

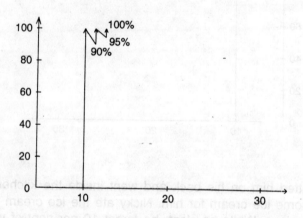

The third day when Nicky went to sleep, his memory level dropped to 95%. Getting up early in the morning, he took up history again! However, this time he was able to reach the optimum level in 15 minutes.

In the pages of his history textbook, he had underlined important words and phrases and what was needed was just to have a look at them. Nicky need not study the subject in depth. He remembered almost everything of what he had studied (95% of ML). What was required was just going through the whole thing again. In short, Nicky was able to complete three revisions in three days, even though the amount of time spent on the second and third revision was only **30 minutes and 15 minutes.**

OBSERVATION CHART

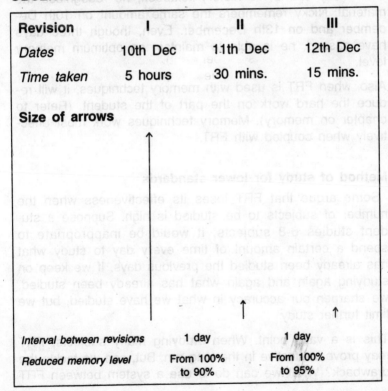

Revision	I	II	III
Dates	10th Dec	11th Dec	12th Dec
Time taken	5 hours	30 mins.	15 mins.
Size of arrows			
Interval between revisions	1 day	1 day	
Reduced memory level	From 100% to 90%	From 100% to 95%	

COMPARATIVE EVALUATION

(a) The taller the arrows, the greater the time and effort required for revision. The tall arrows indicate more time to bring ML to 100 per cent. Since, FRT has shorter arrows, it needs less time and less effort.

(b) The time required for the second and third revision in NRT is 3 hours and 2 hours, while in FRT it is 30 minutes and 15 minutes. Thus it saves time which can be used to study other subjects.

In this chapter, we have closely observed NRT/FRT. We conclude that FRT is a very effective technique of study. The message is that even though you have spent 4-5 hours on a subject for one day, you must spend at least 15-20 minutes studying the same subject the next day. This is to make sure you will not forget what you have learnt. Whenever Nicky opens his history textbook, he recognises the material. Nicky remembers the same amount on 10th December and on 13th December. Even, though three days have passed, he is able to maintain an optimum memory level.

Also, when FRT is used with memory techniques, it will reduce the hard work on the part of the student. (Refer to chapter on memory). Memory techniques work most effectively when coupled with FRT.

Method of study for lower standards

Some argue that FRT loses its effectiveness when the number of subjects to be studied is high. Suppose a student studies 6-8 subjects, it would be inappropriate to spend a certain amount of time every day to study what has already been studied the previous days. If we keep on studying again and again what has already been studied, we sharpen our accuracy in what we have studied, but we limit further study.

This is a valid point. When studying many subjects, FRT may prove ineffective in the long run. But, can we tackle the drawback? What we can do is use a system between FRT and NRT. It covers the positive features of FRT without taking too much time.

A survey revealed that most students follow the method of study mentioned below:

If they have six subjects to study, they take each subject in a row from Monday to Saturday.

Monday: Subject 1
Tuesday: Subject 2
Wednesday: Subject 3
Thursday: Subject 4
Friday: Subject 5
Saturday: Subject 6
Sunday: 'No Study'

Shirley follows this technique. She studies English every Monday. The number of days between two consecutive English revisions is seven days (one whole week.) If she studies geography every Tuesday, the number of days between two consecutive geography revisions is also seven. Thus, every subject is repeated after a week. This is a long gap.

What Shirley can do is given below:

Monday: Subject 1 and Subject 2
Tuesday: Subject 3 and Subject 4
Wednesday: Subject 5 and Subject 6
Thursday: Subject 1 and Subject 2
Friday: Subject 3 and Subject 4
Saturday: Subject 5 and Subject 6

In this case, every subject repeats itself after three days. If English is studied on Monday, it is again studied on Thursday. If history is studied on Tuesday, it is studied again on Friday. Thus, the gap between two consecutive revisions of any subject is just three days. From the point of view of FRT, if we are revising subjects at a gap of three days, we will be able to decrease our efforts in the long run and be able to maintain a stable memory level.

When we study one subject a day, the gap between two

revisions is seven days. When we study two subjects a day, the gap between two revisions is only three days.

There is one more advantage of studying two subjects in a day. If we feel bored of studying any one subject, we can switch to the other subject. This avoids monotony. If one gets bored of studying history, one can switch to maths for some time and then go back to History.

Students in higher standards will find it awkward to study two subjects a day. In higher standards, each subject requires thought and in-depth study. There is more material for study. At two subjects a day the progress will be very slow. It is advisable for them to study one subject for a day but see that the gap between two consecutive revisions does not exceed one week.

Every one of us has a different method of study. We are used to it and it has proved to be very efficient for us in the past. If you have a good method already, do continue with it. Now that you understand the reasoning behind methods of study, you can use it to improve your method.

If I were to summarise the whole chapter in one sentence, I would say:

Try to keep your memory level at the 'just studied' state. Maintain this state of mind until your examinations.

5. SPEED READING, WRITING AND TYPING

'Writing is the best practice.' We have heard this saying from our elders. It is something that has always been stressed by parents and something that children have always ignored.

In my meetings with students who have performed exceptionally in academics, I found that most of them stressed the need of writing practice.

Said Kevin, "Writing practice really pays, because that is exactly what we are going to do in our tests, i.e., write down the answers."

Another friend Joel said, "In today's competitive world every bit of extra knowledge that you show does help." Joel always wrote down in his book what he had learnt. Then, he would go through it as if a moderator/supervisor was assessing his papers and would rate himself. Often, he said, "I was really surprised to see how much I had missed out even though I thought I knew it very well." It is only when you write down that you realise that you have left out many vital things.

In St. Anne's High School, Mumbai, the principal Fr. Ronald Braganza taught us a three-point programme to remember what was learnt.
(a) Reading the text/matter.
(b) Closing the book and trying to recollect it.
(c) Writing it down.

And this three-point method did help me a lot.

It taught me how to arrange my ideas to create maximum impression on the examiner/moderator.

We cannot see the board papers of merit rankers, but it is true that in these papers, there is not a single cancellation. It shows accuracy and perfection that can only come after a great deal of hard work. The ideas are presented systematically. Each thought follows another in a step-by-step, systematic way.

Many students complain that writing is a tedious process and takes a lot of time. I agree. Writing is time-consuming. Writing again and again makes us lose interest in the subject. It is a cumbersome process. Also, it greatly reduces our study time. If we do not write anything for the day than we can study for many more hours on that day. But if we do write for long hours, we have that much less time for study.

A chartered accountant, who was 44th in the CA merit list, shared with me his method of study. In his junior college, during a summer break, he had learnt Pitman's shorthand course. He studied it for an hour a day for three months. This is what people call speed writing, because the course enables you to write 50 to 90 words per minute.

He used to prepare all his notes in shorthand. It is simple as well as easy to understand. He saved a lot of time. Shorthand is a system of writing words and phrases in symbols. Many senior students use shorthand to write down what their teachers teach in the classroom. You can teach yourself shorthand out of a book or through coaching classes.

I have given below 10 general words from the dictionary and also written them in shorthand.

1. Competent
2. Conductor
3. Commissioners
4. Magnificent
5. Self-possession
6. Illiberal
7. Sealing-wax
8. Self-congratulation
9. Accompanying
10. Introducing

When you practice solving question papers, of course, you should not use shorthand because you cannot use it in the actual examination.

SPEED TYPING

Many of you use PCs. Probably even your homework is done on your PC. This is a common sight among the students of advanced countries in the west. Online learning may become common soon. Learn to type fast on your keyboard. There are people who can teach you to type fast or you can install software like Type Tutor or any others that are available. Fast typing will help you throughout your life. You can easily type at 30 wpm (words per minute). After practice you will go up to 40 wpm, 50 wpm, and even 60 wpm. It has also become possible to speak to the computer. (Specific software is designed which automatically types into the computer what you speak. Using such software can greatly help you to reduce time.)

SPEED READING

For students 'where academics is concerned', speed reading can be useful as well as useless. The textbook must be read not only once but many times. Since the textbook is studied in depth, speed reading does not apply to it. But if you are reading any reference or general material related to your subject, you can use speed reading techniques. Your reading speed is measured in 'words per minute' (WPM). The normal reading speed is 240 words per minute. With a little training, it can be improved to 360 wpm and to 600 wpm with more training.

Speed reading requires proper co-ordination between your eyes, which read the subject matter and your 'brain', which interprets the subject matter. It requires a proper co-ordination between your sensory and mental faculties.

According to the science of reading, our eyes move at 'jerks' while reading and not continuously. At each jerk, we are able to grasp the matter. The fewer the jerks while reading the faster you are able to read. Let us take the example of a sentence,

If a/ person paints/ houses/ he is called/ a painter/.

(Every slash denotes a jerk)

If your eyes take five jerks to read the sentence, you are slow. To increase your speed of reading, you have to decrease the number of jerks.

If a person paints houses/ he is called/ a painter.

To reduce the number of jerks you can take a group of words at a time. Let us take one more example. Read this sentence pronouncing each word at a time.

If / a / reader / reads / very / slowly / word / by /word / he / will / be / classified / as / an / inefficient / reader / even / though / he / may / do / well / in / comprehension.

Now, read the same sentence taking the following breaks as suggested:

If a reader / reads very slowly / word by word / he will be / classified as / an inefficient reader / even though / he may / do well / in comprehension.

There are some barriers to speed-reading such as vocalisation, sub-vocalisation and regression.

VOCALISATION

If we murmur or even move our lips while reading, it will reduce our speed. The speed at which we speak is obviously lower than the speed at which we read. For effective comprehension, we have to make a habit of reading aloud every word.

SUB VOCALISATION

Sub-vocalization is inner speech. There is no movement of body parts such as lips or mouth or even the vocal chords. One is not reading aloud, but is pronouncing the words in his mind. If you hear in your mind what you have read in the book, it will reduce your speed. You hear the sound of each word in your mind. Even that partial hearing decreases your speed of reading.

REGRESSION

We often get a sense, while reading, we have missed out a word or a phrase. We go back and forth in search of that missed word. This is called regression. It greatly reduces the flow and speed of reading. The important thing to remember is not go back again and again to find the missed word but cultivate a habit of steady reading.

These are the three main barriers to speed reading. If a student wants to overcome them, it is suggested by experts that initially he should read material of interest to him. After practice, he can read other matter.

So, this was my short introduction to speed writing, speed typing and speed reading. These three important arts can be developed at a very early age. They have many practical applications. These three tools will give you a cutting edge in today's competitive world.

❑❑

6. DEVELOP A PERFECT MEMORY

There are two main reasons why a student gets poor scores in his test. The first reason is that he has not studied the subject matter properly, and the second reason is that he did study but forgot the subject matter he had learnt. Well, if you have not studied the subject matter properly, then, I cannot help you, But if you cannot recollect what you have studied, then this section on memory will be of immense help to you. Not only in your examinations but it will help you throughout your life. The reason being that a good memory is an asset whether you are a student, a parent, a salesman, a business executive or a professional. A good memory will always increase your efficiency at work.

There are some essential requirements of a good memory. If you possess them, they will definitely increase the pace at which you improve your memory. The first requirement is a keen desire for a better memory. You must want to improve your retention and recollection power. The desire should come from within. If it does not, no one can help you.

The second essential requirement is observation. You must in the first place *notice* a certain name, telephone number, etc. If it does not register in your mind, how can you recollect it? You must notice it so that you can remember it. This means that you must be observant. Observe things carefully and try to remember them.

THE CALENDAR FOR THE YEAR 2002

You can use this stunt to impress your friends. This technique will enable you to give the day of the week for any date in the year 2002. The reason I have included it here is that if you are preparing annual plans for study you can use it. To find out on which day your examination starts or ends you can use this technique.

The key is

6 3 3 7 5 2 7 4 1 6 3 1

Each number shows the date on which the first Sunday of that month falls. It simply means that the first Sunday of January falls on the date 6 and the first Sunday of February falls on date 3, the first Sunday of June falls on the date 2 etc.

Effectively, you simply have the whole calendar in front of you. If you want to find the day for any date of the year you can use it.

What is the day on 7th of August?

Since, August is the eighth month of the year, we use the eighth digit in the key. The eighth digit that represents August is 4. We know that it represents the first Sunday of the individual month. As 4th is a Sunday, 7th is a Wednesday.

On which day does Christmas fall in the year 2002?

1 represents December. December 1 is a Sunday. This means that the 8th, 15th and 22nd are Sundays. So, 25th December is a Wednesday. Thus, Christmas falls on Wednesday in the year 2002.

What day is 15th June?

The sixth number in the key, which represents June, is 2. So, 2nd June, 9th June and 16th June are Sundays, and 15th June is a Saturday.

So, you see how simple it is to learn the whole calendar of any year. At the beginning of each year, take up a calendar and make a note of the dates of the first Sundays of each month. This is the key to the entire calendar. The key for the year 2003 is 5 2 2 6 4 1 6 3 7 5 2 7.

We will now study the three essential laws of remembering on which the two most widely used memory systems; the chain system and the piece system are based.

THE FIRST LAW

The first law says that we think in pictures and not in words. If I tell you to imagine a beach, a coconut palm swaying in the breeze and small children building sand castles you will actually see the picture in your mind. You will actually see small children building sand castles. You will not think in words that 'a coconut palm is swaying' Instead you will see it. This is the first law, we *think in pictures.*

THE SECOND LAW

The second law states that we remember only that which makes sense to us. We forget nonsense. Read this sentence and repeat it, 'komrichawsaki tupulutu sehjikeop chuisrtuow' Repeat it loudly without looking at it; you will find that it is practically impossible to repeat it because you cannot understand it. Now read this sentence, 'The Statue of Liberty is in New York.' Repeat it right now. The Statue of Liberty is in New York. This means something to us, whether or not we knew it beforehand, and so we are able to repeat it.

THE THIRD LAW

The third law states that we easily remember special things. The conscious brain does not remember something that is routine and generally seen everywhere. The special and the unique makes us curious, it attracts our attention, we notice it and we remember it. If I tell you to recollect what you did on 14th August 1997, you will not remember it. You cannot remember the routine of your whole life. Instead, if I ask you what you did on New Year's eve, especially December 31, 2000, you will be able to tell me. The simple reason being it was a special and unique event. We remember events like our birthdays simply because they were *special.*

Combining the three laws, we get one single principle that is the foundation of all memory techniques. 'We remember special pictures which are sensible.' (These techniques depend on understanding how the human brain works.)

Almost any text matter that we desire to remember must be

sensible, special to us and then should be converted into mental pictures so that it can be remembered. We can make it special by making it illogical and impossible.

Given below is a list of ten words which we shall call the temporary list.

THE TEMPORARY LIST

Look at the list

One is bun
Two is shoe
Three is tree
Four is door
Five is hive
Six is sticks
Seven is heaven
Eight is gate
Nine is wine
Ten is den

This is the temporary piece list which you have to remember. It is based on these ten words that you will associate what you have to remember. Read the list once again. You will notice that each word rhymes with the number associated with it. Thus, we can remember it.

Read the list given above three times. Now look at the following list of words and try to memorise them.

1. Watch
2. Feathers
3. Book
4. Computer
5. Pen
6. Shirt
7. Car
8. Biscuit
9. Airplane
10. Flag

You can use your own way of remembering it, but you will fail. Now, use the piece system and see how effective it is!

In the first list, a word is given with a number. In the second list, another word is given against the same number. We combine both the lists to form a picture.

- One is bun. One is also watch. View yourself wearing a bun instead of a watch.

- Two is shoe. Two is also feathers. Visualize feathers sprouting from your shoes.

- Three is tree. Three is also book. Visualise your library full of trees.

- Four is door. Four is also a computer. Imagine your house having a computerised locking system.

- Five is hive. Five is also pen. Think of bees flying around your pen.

- Six is sticks. Six is also shirt. Think of wearing a shirt made of sticks.

- Seven is heaven. Seven is also car. See yourself driving a car in the clouds.

- Eight is gate. Eight is also biscuits. Remember Hansel and Gretel, and the witch's house whose door was made of biscuits.

- Nine is wine. Nine is also an airplane. Imagine drinking airplanes out of a bottle.

- Ten is den. Ten is also flag. Visualise a lion's den with your country's flag outside it.

Read all the ten points once again. Read them until you are confident of your imagined associations. Now try to write them down from ten to one. I repeat, from ten to one, even though I know we have learnt it from one to ten.

- Ten—Den, Den has a flag. Ten is *flag*.

- Nine—wine. Wine is in a bottle. From the bottles airplanes are flying out. Nine is *airplanes*.

- Eight—gate. Gate of a witch's house. The gate has biscuits. Eight is *biscuits*.

- Seven—heaven. Heaven is up in the clouds. Yes, a car is flying in the clouds. Seven is a *car*.

- Six—sticks. Sticks are on your shirt. Six is a *shirt*.

- Five—hive. A hive has bees. But bees are flying around your pen. Five is *pen*.

- Four—door. A computerised door. Four is a *computer*.

- Three—tree. Trees are in your library. But the library is made of books. Three is *books*.

- Two—shoe. But the shoes have feathers sprouting out of them. Two is *feathers*.

- One—bun. The bun is on your wrist where you wear a watch. One is *watch*.

Now try to write down the words in the order given without refering to the list.

7.

3.

8.

1.

4.

10.

2.

5.

6.

9.

Check whether the answers are correct. Even if there are mistakes, don't worry. This was your first attempt. You will improve to the level of near-perfect recall.

The advantage of piece system is that you can forget any list whenever you want and replace it with a new list. Suppose I give you ten more words and tell you to remember them, you can easily associate each of them with the pieces. When the second list is given to you, the first list is easily forgotten.

Here, I have given you only 10 words, just for an initial demo to show you how the system works. Experts can memorise 100 words within 3-5 minutes. You can increase the number of words you memorise as you progress. For the time being, be satisfied with ten words, because it is no small achievement.

Next we will take up the conversion system of memory. Meanwhile, enjoy giving demonstrations to your friends.

Tell them to write numbers from 1 to 10 and against each number an object of their choice. After they have written the list, take the paper in your hand. Memorise them.

Tell your friends that you can repeat the 10 words in the correct or reverse order, whichever they prefer. Show them both, go from 1 to 10 and 10 to 1. Then, ask them to give you a number and tell them the word against that number.

THE CONVERSION SYSTEM OF MEMORY

We forget numbers. Numbers are not remembered for a long times. To show you what I mean, let us take an example. Given alongside is a sentence, which you have to read once, and then repeat it in your mind without looking at it. The sentence is 'Canada is a beautiful and a peace-loving country.' Now, repeat the sentence without looking at it. You will find that you were able to do so. As a second part of my example, look at the series of numbers given below just once and repeat all the numbers in a row without looking at them.

'82539648562749'

Were you able to repeat the number exactly without looking at them? You were not. Many numbers put together side by side do not make any sense. Simply because our three laws of memory say that we remember only sensible stuff that can be viewed as a picture.

In the conversion system, we convert every number into a

letter of the English alphabet. We have assigned a letter or letters from the English alphabet to each number. The number 1 has been assigned the letters N and B. The number two has been assigned the letters H and S and so on. The complete list is given below.

1 - B, N (Remember One = **B**u**N**. So, the letters allocated to 1 are B and N)

2 - W, S

3 - T (Three = **T**ea)

4 - D, R (Four = **D**oo**R**)

5 - L, V (Five = **L**i**V**e)

6 - C, K (Six = sti**CK**)

7 - M (2 seven's written sideways make an **M**)

8 - G, F (*g* and *f* both resemble 8)

9 - P (**p** resembles 9 when seen in the mirror)

0 - J, H

We have not allocated the letters A, E, I, O, U and Q, X, Y, Z to any numbers.

The conversion system of memory helps you remember anything associated with numbers. Students studying history have dates to remember, and those studying geography and economics have statistics. Everybody has a need to remember telephone numbers. In such cases, the conversion system of memory does help. Since, it is based on the piece system of memory, I advise you to learn the pieces from 1 to 0.

A lot of numbers together do not make sense by themselves. Even if you read them many times, there is no certainty that you will remember them. The conversion system of memory helps us remember them. Numbers are converted into words (which make sense) and the words give us a picture we can hold in our minds.

TELEPHONE NUMBERS

The conversion system of memory has helped me easily

memorise the telephone numbers of around 300 people, each of 7 digits. It is not that I do not have the use of a telephone diary, but learning the habit and practice of memorising definitely improves my ability to remember dates, chemical formulae, statistics and sections of various laws and acts when I study economics. It helps me when I give memory demonstrations.

If you remember the names and phone numbers of people, they are happy that you are giving them importance, even though that may not be the case. This will make your relations more friendly. People in the corporate world fear that when they meet a person they may find that they have forgotten his name. We generally do not forget faces; only the names are forgotten. If you remember the phone numbers of your friends, they will be very happy.

Here's the phone number of my friend Pintu – 4963812. This was the first number I learnt using the conversion technique. The piece for 4 is R, for 9 is P, for 6 is C and so on. Thus, the number 4963812 will be represented by the digits RPCTFNS. Since, we can insert vowels, the words formed are RoPe CaT FaNS.

4 R	6 C	8 F
9 P	3 T	1 N
		2 S
(RoPe)	(CaT)	(FaNS)

This phone number belongs to my friend. So, whenever I see him, I imagine that a **cat** has tied his legs with a **rope** and the cat has hung him upside down with his two legs tied to two different **fans**. Whenever I see him, this picture flashes in my mind and I remember the words rope, cat and fans. This reminds me that his phone number is 4963812.

Let us take the example of another phone number. The phone number is 659381. Assume it belongs to your friend. Make sure you use the name of a real friend. Use the conversion technique.

Using the standard pieces, we have

$$6 = C \qquad 9 = P \qquad 8 = G$$
$$5 = V \qquad 3 = T \qquad 1 = N$$

(**C** a **V** e)   (**P** o **T**)   (**G** u **N**)

See your friend sitting inside a cave, with a pot below him and with a gun over his head. Here, we can imagine him carrying a gun in his hand instead of carrying it over his head. But since we are trying to make the picture more unique following the third law of remembering, we imagine him carrying a gun over his head.

The basic idea is to convert meaningless numbers into meaningful pictures so that we can remember them.

Let us move to the example of case laws. Students of law, accountancy, economics, taxation and other such subjects, need to learn the sections, acts, and amendments in the laws of their respective countries. For their help, I have prepared an imaginary extract of a country's constitution. Imagine the six sections mentioned below apply to the citizens of a country and assume that they will be punished on that basis.

SECTION	PUNISHMENT
451	To be hanged till death.
452	No punishment
453	10 years imprisonment
454	Imprisonment for life
455	Penalty of 100 Rs.
456	Cancellation of foreign visas

Imagine these six sections dealing with six different sorts of punishments. Now, think of a way to learn them. You can probably learn them by your traditional method of remembering and it may work. But think about actual law books. Their sheer size and number of pages is daunting. There are thousands of sections and sub-sections and sub-sub-sections that deal with all types of crimes, offences etc.

65

Of course you need a scientific approach to learn them and that is none other than the conversion system of memory.

Just watch how the conversion system comes to your aid.

If 4 is R, 5 is V and 1 is N, then 451 is RVN. Thus, we can insert vowels and make 451 - Raven. Raven is a bird. Imagine a bird carrying you in its beak until you die. Thus, section 451 will remind you that it stands for 'to be hanged till death.'

452 - RaiLS. Think of yourself sleeping on the railway lines, a train moving over you and yet you are safe and sound. Nothing bad happens to you. This reminds you that section 452 stands for no punishment.

453 - DeLTa (of a river). Imagine yourself caught in a river such that you cannot get out alive. You are imprisoned in it for life.

454 - RuLeR. Imagine a 10 centimetre or 10 inch ruler or scale. Thus, it is associated with the fact that section 454 means ten years of imprisonment.

455 - DeViL. Imagine a devil grabbing hold of your neck and saying he will not let go unless you give him 100 Rs. Thus it reminds you that you have to pay a fine of a 100 Rs to be freed.

456 - eDVaC. EDVAC was a type of a computer. See in your mind a computer showing an error message that it will not process your visas. Thus, 456 is cancellation of foreign visas.

The list is really basic and simple. In actuality it has nothing to do with law, or any other specific subject. For this reason it can be applied to any subject.

The conversion method helps us reduce the time and effort spent in learning and also makes it more interesting. It makes you attack your study material from a totally different angle. A perspective that promises 'no forgetting'. You can try it out for yourself. Check whether you remember it after reading it twice. When you have read it over two or three different days that 456 is cancellation of foreign visas, you will never forget it. Initially, you will have to think of the computer that is not accepting your visas, but after two or three readings you will automatically think of your foreign visas being cancelled when you come across the number 456 without the thought of the computer.

HOW TO REMEMBER DATES IN HISTORY

Many students have a problem remembering dates in History. The reason is that there are so many dates to remember, and students do not use **any** system. The technique that I use to remember dates is the conversion technique. Here, it will make no difference whether there are a few dates or more because you will never forget them.

Let us take the example of a few dates. Along with the dates, I have given you the name of the event that took place on that particular date.

1912 - The sinking of Titanic
1947 - The independence of India
1914 - Beginning of World War I
1953 - Everest first conquered by man
1674 - Death of John Milton, the poet

Now, let us see how we will memorise these dates. They are arranged randomly. Since, 1 is common in all these dates, we will not consider 1 but consider the remaining digits of the date.

In 1912, we will consider only 912 and in 1674, we will consider only 674.

According to our standard conversion list, 9 is P, 1 is N and 2 is S.

9 - p
1 - n
2 - s

912 - **P** I **N** **S**

Since the event associates with the date 1912 is the sinking of the Titanic, you can visualise the Titanic sinking into a sea of pins. You could imagine a pinprick deflating a life jacket. So, whenever you see the word Titanic in the examination paper, you will see a 'sea of PiNS' and remember that it sank in 1912.

9 - p
4 - d
7 - m

947 - **P O D I U M**

The event associated with the year 1947 is the freedom of India from the British. Think of little children performing a play on a stage (podium) and finally the Indian flag is hoisted. Or you can think of anything that makes the picture more special and illogical.

Again,

9 - p
1 - n
4 - d

(914 - **P O N D**)

Visualise a lot of people fighting each other in a pond. These people are wearing military outfits that have the number 1 written behind it, and so it suggests World War 1.

9 - p
5 - l
3 - t

(953 - **P I L O T**)

Visualise a pilot climbing a mountain dragging a plane behind him. Thus, Mt. Everest will remind you of a pilot which will bring to mind 1953.

6 - c
7 - m
4 - r

(674 - **C A M E R A**)

Visualise a coffin in which the dead body of John Milton has been kept. The coffin is in the shape of a camera. You may wonder how can you visualise John Milton when you do not know what he looked like. You do not have to bother about his looks. Just remember the coffin shaped like a camera and that is enough.

Using the conversion system, it is even possible to remember specific dates like 14th September 1984, 25th November 1978, etc. There are ways to do it. You can develop your own ways to remember them.

If you have a few dates to learn, you do not need to convert them. But, if you have to learn many dates, it is always advisable to have a definite and scientific approach. That is where the need to use the conversion system of memory arises.

This is how you can remember dates in History. Though this seems a tedious task, believe me, even if there are some hundred dates in your history book, you can easily convert all of them in a day's time. Keep this book with you and the book can be used for reference throughout the year. At the end of the year, pass it on to another student.

THE CHAIN SYSTEM OF MEMORY

The chain system of memory is used in memory demonstrations, remembering speeches and articles and very importantly to remember our answers. It should be noted here that I do not recommend blindly mugging up the answers in the textbook. Use a scientific approach such as the chain system. Never will I advise blind memorization because that never helps. Blind memorization is only temporary knowledge and it never helps in the long run.

As an initial exercise, memorize this list of seven words.

Radio
Bottle
Pen
Shoes
Spectacles
Banana skin
Mouse

Now, you have to learn the words in a line and not in a

random manner. Then, how will you go about doing it? The chain system is the scientific approach for remembering the list. In the chain system, we link the first item in the list to the second item, the second item to the third item and so on. If you link the words using the directions provided below it will be easier for you to memorise.

ILLOGICAL ASSOCIATION

Two consecutive items should be linked in such a manner that the picture formed is illogical. Yes, if it is too natural you will easily forget it because it is such a common thing. Assume you have to link chair to pizza. If you visualise yourself eating the pizza while sitting on a chair, it is pretty ordinary and may not be retained. On the other hand, if you visualise a chair eating a pizza, it will definitely be remembered because it is illogical.

ACTION

Imagine the linked association to be 'an action.' It gives a sense of happening to the picture and can be retained easily. It is like a movie that is running in your mind's eye. Visualise a chair reaching out with its two hands (arms rests) and eating the pizza.

PERSONIFICATION

Personification means giving to an object a human quality, expression or emotion. It is giving an inanimate object life and intelligence. In the above example, how about a wicked chair eating a pizza voraciously.

So, the three factors that must be kept in mind before linking are illogical association, action and personification.

Let us see how you can memorise the list of seven words.

1. Visualise yourself drinking water out of a radio (instead of a bottle).

2. Visualise yourself writing from a bottle (instead of a pen).

3. Now, you are wearing pens on you feet (instead of shoes).

4. You are wearing shoes on your eyes (instead of spectacles).

5. If you walk on your spectacles, you will slip. This reminds you of a banana skin.

6. You are using a banana skin to double-click, which is actually done by the mouse. Thus, banana-skin will give you mouse.

The important thing here is to see the picture in your mind's eye. You must *see* the picture. Because we are doing it for the first time, let us do it once again. Go through the whole list once again. After reading every statement, close your eyes and visualise it.

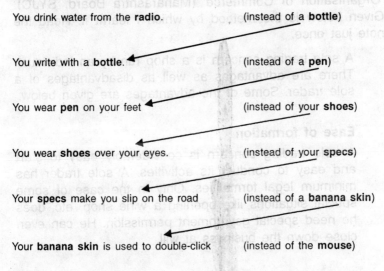

You drink water from the **radio**.   (instead of a **bottle**)

You write with a **bottle**.   (instead of a **pen**)

You wear **pen** on your feet   (instead of your **shoes**)

You wear **shoes** over your eyes.   (instead of your **specs**)

Your **specs** make you slip on the road   (instead of a **banana skin**)

Your **banana skin** is used to double-click   (instead of the **mouse**)

Thus

Radio → Bottle → Pen → Shoes → Spectacles → Banana skin → Mouse

You can see that in the chain system of memory, one item

leads to the next as in a chain. All the individual items act as the links of the chain and therefore some memory experts call it the **link** system of memory.

Now, you can write down the seven words without looking at them:

1.
2.
3.
4.
5.
6.
7.

APPLICATIONS OF MEMORY SYSTEMS

EXAMPLE 1

I have reproduced below a note related to the subject 'Organisation of Commerce' (Maharashtra Board, SYJC). Given below is the method by which I learnt it. Read the note just once.

A sole trading concern is a shop run by an individual. There are advantages as well as disadvantages of a sole trader. Some of the advantages are given below.

Ease of formation

A sole trading concern is considerably easy to start and easy to conduct its activities. A sole trader has minimum legal formalities. Only in the case of some special situations like opening a wine shop, etc. does he need special government permission. He can even close down the business at will.

Business Secrecy

A joint stock company has to publish its annual accounts and other legal formalities. A sole trader is not bound to do so. It is difficult for his competitors to obtain information about him.

72

Flexibility of operation

A sole trader can change his line of business whenever he wants. He can even shut down his work as per his wishes. If a job is not going well for him, he can change it.

Limited tax liability

A sole trader has to pay a limited amount of tax as compared to big firms. He need not disclose his entire business income to outside parties.

Better relations with customers

A sole trader can directly sell the goods to the customer. The owner of a joint stock company does not come face to face with the customers. Thus, a sole trader can establish personal relations with customers.

As I have stressed earlier, we are not interested in blindly mugging up the answers, we just want to remember the main points. The rest of the details can be expanded on our own.

The five main points are:

Ease of formation,
Business secrecy,
Flexibility of operation,
Limited tax liability, and
Better relations with customers.

Let us recall the temporary list for our help.

- One is bun. One is also ease of formation. See buns being made very easily at a hotel.

- Two is shoe. Two is also business secrecy. Visualise one shoe whispering to another.

- Three is tree. It is also flexibility of operation. Visualise a very flexible tree. You can bend it in all directions.

73

- Four is door. It is limited tax liability. Visualise a tax officer knocking at the door and the door giving him only a single coin.

- Five is hive. Visualise honeybees selling honey to human beings and shaking hands with them. The human beings are the customers.

Now, read the list once again and see if you can remember the points. You will be successful.

Isn't it easy and exciting! It makes studies such a lot of fun. My friends to whom I have taught these techniques often exchange their funny ideas and imaginings. That is why I am sure children will love this idea. Education can be a lovely experience or a bore depending on how you view it. I would like to encourage teachers, parents, students and everyone else to follow these techniques and pass them on to others. You may think that it takes a lot of time to prepare links, but actually it does not. When I explain these things, I must go slow. Once you get the knack of it, you will be able to do it fast.

You can keep the chains, pieces ready in a separate log-book and they can be used for LMR – Last Minute Revision – just before your examinations. Pass this book on to your friends. You can even share out among a group of students the job of forming chains or pieces.

EXAMPLE 2

This is an extract from the geography textbook for Standard 10 (Maharashtra Board). The method can be used for any subject.

THE INDIAN PLATEAU

The Indian plateau is a triangular shaped, **ancient**, stable landmass. It is surrounded by the Aravalli hills in the west and the Rajmahal hills in the east. In the south are the Nilgiri Mountains (the Nilgiri mountains are called the blue mountains). In the east are broken ranges of the Eastern Ghats while in the west are the

broken ranges of the Western Ghats. The Narmada
and Tapi rivers flow through the North Indian Plateau.'

Convert every important and non-understood fact into
something that can be made into pictures and remembered.
This is one way of doing it.

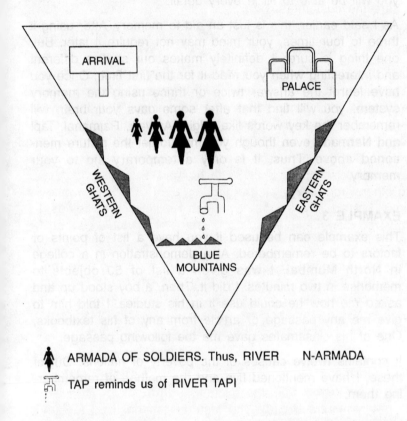

ARMADA OF SOLDIERS. Thus, RIVER   N-ARMADA

TAP reminds us of RIVER TAPI

Every minute detail in the picture has its significance. The
plateau is made triangular. It looks very **ancient** (Black and
white). The 'arrival board' reminds us of the Aravalli Mountains. The palace reminds us of the Rajmahal hills because
the word Rajmahal means the palace of a king. The Blue
Mountains remind us of the Nilgiris. Similarly, the broken
ranges on both the sides signify the Western and Eastern
Ghats. Inside the plateau is a tap that is giving out water.
The tap reminds us of the river Tapi. Also, visualise a fleet

of soldiers in the plateau. A fleet of soldiers makes up an Armada. Thus, river N-Armada.

Look at the picture carefully for some time and read the explanation. Visualise every detail. This picture is just to remind you of the main things. After some days of revision, you will be able to fill in every detail.

As I said earlier, this is just an aid to memory. After using it three to four times, your mind may not require it later. But, one thing is sure; it definitely makes our studies different and interesting when you read it for the first time. Once you have learnt the answer twice or thrice using the memory system, you will find that after some days your brain will remember the key words like Nilgiri, Aravalli, Rajmahal, Tapi and Narmada even though you may forget the picture mentioned above. Thus, it is only a temporary aid to your memory.

EXAMPLE 3

This example can be used if you have a list of points or factors to be remembered. At a demonstration in a college in North Mumbai, I was given a list of 50 objects to memorise in two minutes. I did it. Then, a boy stood up and asked me how he could use it in his studies. I told him to give me any passage or article from any of his textbooks. One of his classmates gave me the following passage.

It contains twelve causes of the poverty of nations. Out of these, I have mentioned five and the method of remembering them.

The Five Causes of the Poverty of Nations
1. Population
2. Illiteracy
3. Unemployment
4. Poor development of science
5. Natural calamities

You can remember this list using the chain system.

76

Visualise many, many poor people (overpopulation). They are all reading newspapers. But, they cannot understand anything; they can only see the pictures (illiteracy). You must actually see in your mind that the people are reading the newspapers. **See it now**. In the newspaper, there is a photograph of a big boss. He is bald and has big moustache. He suddenly comes out of the newspaper. He tells the people that they are removed from their job (unemployment). Now the people are fired, and so they start making a fire! (What a stupid comparison! People are fired so they start making a fire. But it is this stupid comparison that will help you remember things). They have to use flint stones to make the fire because they do not have matchsticks (lack of scientific development). Somehow they make up a fire using flint-stones. But suddenly it starts raining heavily. The fire, people and their household, everything is washed off (natural calamities).

Thus, all our five points are covered in the form of a story.

Many poor people remind us of population.
Inability to read newspapers reminds us of illiteracy.
The boss firing the people reminds us of unemployment.
The flint stones remind us of 'poor development of science'.
And the heavy rain reminds us of natural calamities.

We actually see the events in our mind. If you go through this story three times on three consecutive days, you may never need to read it again.

I called the boy who had asked me to do this task. He was reluctant initially, but I was able to interest him. I told the audience how I memorised the first five points. Then I asked him to memorise all 12. And believe me, when we tested him he had got all 12 points right. He had formed a very interesting and funny story of the twelve points. Though he took time, as it was his first attempt, I am sure regular use will increase his speed – and your speed too.

EXAMPLE 4

In all these examples, I have given a different way to remember the answer keeping in mind our memory systems.

So just go through every example very slowly and try to grasp the method used for remembering. Each example is different. The paragraph given below deals with the measures for control of air pollution. To remember it what we do is take the main words from each sentence and link them. Take the main word from each sentence and link it with the main word of the next sentence and so on. But as far as possible try to take that main word which will help you to form a picture in your mind. Given below is a paragraph written in a point form and the main words are underlined. To remember the whole answer we take the main words and form a chain using the chain system already explained.

Measures for Control of Air Pollution

- *Tall chimneys* in factories help to discharge pollutants at the high altitudes.

- *Automobiles* should be checked regularly as regards complete combustion of fuels.

- *Green vegetation* around industry seems to be a good solution to reduce pollution.

- If the use of a *raw material* produces more pollution a suitable one should replace it.

- People should be educated using mass media like *television* etc.

A main word or main words are such words in the sentence that can convey the meaning of the whole sentence. They are the important words, which can remind you of the whole sentence.

The main words in each point are:

Tall chimneys,
Automobiles,
Green vegetation,
Raw material, and
Television.

Now, we need to link all of them in order to form one whole

chain. The first word is linked to the second and the second is linked to the third and so on.

First we need to link tall chimneys with automobiles. Visualise some tall chimneys and from each one of them 'automobiles are flying out.'

Now we need to link automobiles with green vegetation. Visualise that when these automobiles fall on the ground, many green trees start growing on the spots where they fell.

Now, we need to link green vegetation to raw material. We can definitely see a picture of green vegetation, but how do we see the picture of a raw material? Well, since we already have the word 'green vegetation' with us, we use the picture of a raw mango to represent raw material. Now, to link raw material with green vegetation, we visualise that raw mangoes are falling down from the trees that have grown from the automobiles.

Finally, we need to link raw material with television. This is simple. Imagine yourself going and picking up a raw mango. When you cut it open with a knife, a television set emerges out of it.

The whole movie goes this way.

Automobiles are flying out of chimneys; they fall on the ground and trees start growing out of them. Raw mangoes start falling from the trees. When you cut one, you find a television set.

Tall chimneys → Automobiles → Green vegetation → Raw material → Television.

Just go through the movie a few times seeing it in your mind's eye. When you write down the answer in your examination, the points start flowing in your mind that first you need tall chimneys to discharge pollution in high altitudes, then you need to grow green vegetation, if raw material causes pollution then replace it and finally educate people through the use of mass media.

Simple, isn't it?

Always remember to link the main words when you need to

memorise this type of data. When you have to remember speeches and big articles, what you can do is underline the main words from each paragraph of the speech and form a chain.

- Write down the speech.
- Read three to four times until you are very familiar with what it says.
- Then underline the main words.
- If you have ten main words in your speech, then write down the ten main words one below the other.
- Link them to form a chain.

If you are giving the speech, you may be saying something related to the first main word, and that brings the second main word to mind. This process continues until you finish your speech. One main word follows the other and then the next and so on.

Again, as usual the focus is not on learning the speech by rote but remembering it. If you memorise it blindly then you may forget it. But, if you do not memorise it, how can you forget it? What we are doing is consciously remembering what we have written down. Make sure to remember the chain properly, because if it is forgotten then you have lost the whole speech.

Public speaking is an art that everyone needs some time or the other. The main reason people are afraid of it is that they are afraid that they might forget the prepared speech and will make fools of themselves before the public.

If you form a link of the main words and remember the chain properly, you will never forget your words. Also, once your main words are in order, you can elaborate on them in any manner you like. You may add a few sentences here and there, or may decide to drop some. The important thing is that the main message is being conveyed and that is what counts. Sometimes, we see people who talk without realising that they are giving a public speech. They have blindly memorised the speech. If they forget word here and there, they just cannot continue. One mistake and everything is lost. If you just vomit out on the stage what you have learnt by rote, your speech will be very boring, dull and dry. Instead, when you are conscious of giving a speech, your words will be as active, alive and vibrant as yourself.

EXAMPLE 5

In these methods, the subject matter learnt is recollected from the conscious brain. Many students get good marks by blindly mugging up answers. They learn by rote until the material registers in their sub-conscious minds. Whenever you ask such a student a particular question, the answer will flow out. But the student will not be thinking of the meanings of the words he speaks. If you wake him in the middle of the night and ask him a question, the answer will flow out of him. My techniques will help you actively remember the subject matter and not blindly memorise it. I always insist that one must 'remember and recollect' and 'not mug up and recollect.'

A memory aid is not required after some time because regular use makes it habitual. You will not need an aid of memory to remind you of anything learnt thoroughly. You will simply remember the subject matter by itself. Let me illustrate this point with an example:

We were taught in school the names of the nine planets in our solar system. As we know they are **M**ercury, **V**enus, **E**arth, **M**ars, **J**upiter, **S**aturn, **U**ranus, **N**eptune, **P**luto. The initial letters are, M V E M J S U N P. Also, all of us were given a sentence to remember the names of these planets. The sentence was,

My **V**ery **E**ducated **M**other **J**ust **S**howed **U**s **N**ine **P**lanets.

We learnt this sentence at a very young age. As time passed on, we did not require the sentence, because we had learnt the order of the planets by then.

I initially learnt the letters of the Greek alphabet using the piece system of memory. As time passed, I could locate the letters without any pieces. With daily use, they had been internalised and did not require any pieces to remember them.

Shopkeepers sell many varieties of articles. They do not need to refer to the price list for the price of every item. Nor do they know the memory techniques. Then how do they remember the prices of all the articles? They know them because of daily use.

Hindu prayers are mostly written in Sanskrit language. Very few children know this language. It is not a language of general conversation but rather a language of study. Children can read Sanskrit but it is slightly difficult for them to understand its meaning on their own. But still they easily memorise two-page long Sanskrit prayers despite the fact that sometimes they do not know the meaning! They remember something that they may not have fully understood. Again the reason is daily recitation.

What we can learn from the above examples is that when something is used daily, or repeatedly, we become less dependent on it's related memory aid.

If we are learning any foreign language, we can use the concept mentioned above. It helps us remember even abstract information. What we do is convert something that we cannot understand into something that we can understand.

To give you an example, the French word for 'day' is 'jour'. You can make a picture of your calendar where all the days of the week are shown by a 'jar.' Thus, jour means day.

The Hindi word for tree is 'ped' (pronounced like 'paid'). You can make a picture of you writing on a tree instead of a pad. (Writing - pad). Thus, tree is ped.

'Acoustics' is the science of sound. You can imagine a cow and a stick coming out of your mouth as you speak (a-cow-stick).

To remember the triangular shape of the bone called 'sacrum', you can imagine a triangular sack that is filled with bottles of rum.

You may ask what if we forget the word 'sacrum' but remember the picture. We know that there is a triangular shaped sack containing bottles of rum. We will think that the correct word is 'rumsac' and not sacrum.

Apart from our trained memory we also have 'natural memory.' It is our natural memory that will help us remember that the correct word is 'sacrum' not 'rumsac'.

Our natural memory is also very powerful. There are so many people who do not use any memory system, but still remember so many things. Their powerful natural memory helps them to do so. We all have a very powerful natural memory. If you learn the memory techniques, you will be providing a back up for your natural memory.

How To Remember Complex Vocabulary

Students appearing for competitive examinations have to spend a lot of time in enhancing their vocabulary. Given below is an example of the substitution system of memory that can be used to remember complex vocabulary. Have a look at the list of words given below:

Dogmatic - inflexible, unbending

Exculpate - absolve from blame

Euphoria - a state of intense excitement or happiness

Ostracise - exclude from a group

Blighted - destroyed, spoilt

Nettle - irritate or annoy or vex

Rail - complain strongly

In the substitution system, we break the complex word whose meaning we do not know into that which we already know.

Let us take the words one by one.

- The first word is 'dogmatic' and it means inflexible. Imagine you have a pet dog in your home and it is very stiff. Thus, whenever you *hear* the word 'dogmatic', it will remind you that it means inflexible.

- The second word is 'exculpate' and it means 'to absolve

83

from blame'. Now, view the word exculpate as ex-culprit. It means that the person was a culprit before and is no more a culprit. Thus, he is 'absolved from blame'.

- Euphoria is a state of intense excitement or happiness. Visualise the Euphoria group (the pop band) dancing and screaming. Thus, Euphoria will remind you that it stands for joy.

- The word ostracise means to exclude. Imagine that all ostriches are banished from society or excluded from the zoo.

- 'Blighted' means 'destroyed'. Visualise yourself as one day you got very angry over something and so you destroyed all the lights in your home. We use the word light because it reminds us of the word blighted.

- Nettle means to irritate or vex. At first glance it seems difficult to substitute the words. But we can substitute both the words. Substitute nettle as nestle and substitute 'to vex' as 'to wax'. Thus, you must visualise a Nestle (brand) bottle made of wax. When you read the word nettle, it will remind you of a Nestle bottle which is made up of wax and so you will remember 'to vex'.

- Rail means to complain strongly and persistently. Imagine that the 'rail'ways are not working properly and you are complaining loudly to the authorities.

Go through this list once again very slowly and then try to write the meanings of the words to test yourself.

Ostracise -
Nettle -
Dogmatic -
Euphoria -
Rail -
Blighted -
Exculpate -

Check the meanings. Most of you will have got more than five correct answers. Anything above four correct answers is good. If you performed poorly, do not worry because practice will improve your performance.

In my memory demonstrations, I get the highest applause when I show students the 50-object method of memory. I ask them to give me the names of any 50 objects. I write down the numbers from 1 to 50 and beside each number I write down the 50 objects that they have given me. Then I recall all the numbers in a line from 1 to 50 or 50 –to 1, or from 40 to 49 without looking at the blackboard and entirely out of my memory. Sometimes, I recall the numbers in any random order or an order given to me by the audience because it makes no difference to me.

Now, even you can do it if you want. You can stun your friends by the way you do it.

Suppose that there are 50 students in your class. Obviously you know their names. Now, try to learn even their roll numbers. When someone asks you to memorise a list of 50 numbers, you associate the first object with the student whose roll number is 1. Relate the second object with the student whose roll number is 2 and so on.

If someone asks you what is the word at number 36, you can immediately tell him the word. You recall the student with roll number 36 and give the answer. If someone asks you what is the word at number 27, you know that your friend Amit has the roll number 27 and you have formed the association that he is very fond of watching 'television' which is the object on the list.

I use this method. There are 50 flats in my building. I associate the first word with my friend staying in flat number 1. The second word with my friend staying in flat number 2 and so on.

You can start with 20 words in the beginning and then increase the number of words. Let us assume that the first five roll numbers in our class are:

M. Jackson - 1
A. Lincoln - 2
M. Gandhi - 3

A. Hitler - 4

W. Shakespeare - 5

We have been asked to remember the list of five words given below:

(1) Hat
(2) Rocket
(3) Pencil
(4) Boat
(5) Telephone

M. Jackson is wearing a hat.

A. Lincoln is controlling a rocket

M. Gandhi is writing with a pencil.

A. Hitler is rowing a boat.

W. Shakespeare is talking on a phone.

Go through the above list three times and write down the words in the blanks given below.

3.

1.

4.

5.

2.

This is what we practised with five words. You may want to test your ability to remember more words. The important thing is to increase your capacity to memorise at a slow and stable pace.

There are many people who can even remember 100 words at a time. The system of memory used to remember 100 words is a modified 'piece' system. It combines the conversion system with the piece system. That is beyond the scope of the book. But there are books available in the market on the subject.

We have studied the different systems of memory. These techniques of memory are very useful. As an individual practices more and more his accuracy will increase at a definite pace. The more you practice the better you become at memorising. You can try this experiment on your friends.

Take a piece of paper and a pen and ask them to write any 25 words of their choice. For example:

(1) Soap
(2) Bell
(3) Camel
(4) Cap
and so on...

After your friends have given you the list, try to memorise it in five minutes using the chain system. Once you have memorised the list, give the paper back to your friends and recite the whole list from 1 to 25. They will be impressed.

Such demonstrations prove very effective. They give you practice and increase your interest in memory systems. This is the first step to becoming a professional memory expert. You can then move on to stage demonstrations and public performances.

FRT AND MEMORY

To use FRT with memory systems, create a separate logbook where you have a lot of readymade chains. Example 1 gives five features of a sole trader. In your logbook write down only the five features without any elaboration.

Thus the five points will read:

- Ease of formation
- Business secrecy
- Flexibility of operation
- Limited tax liability
- Better relations with customers

How will you apply FRT to it? You regularly revise the chains in your logbook. If you revise them once a week, it is enough. Twice a week is excellent. But the gap should not be more than a fortnight. We know that regular revision helps us to maintain a stable memory level.

Students report that after revising the chains in the logbook once a week for four to five weeks, they were able to recall later what they had read six to seven months earlier. When

87

you have learnt so well, you will not require the chain system to remember the list. You will simply remember the order and all the points in every list and that too with ease.

At examination time also, the logbook will help. Instead of scanning pages of the textbook, you can use the logbook as a quick reference. Flipping through the pages of a book creates panic, and panic leads to frustration. If you frequently revise chains, the logbook will be the only thing you need to refer at the time of the examinations.

Refer to example 4. It shows us the control measures of air pollution. There are five main words in it: tall chimneys, automobiles, green vegetation, raw material and television. We have already formed an imaginary movie of these five points and written down the main words in our logbook. Just go through the movie two to three times before the examination and you will remember all the main words when you are writing your paper. The same happens when you are going to give a speech and especially if it is a long one. If you have 15-20 'main words' in your speech, you can try to remember all of them in a chain format just a few minutes before you actually walk up on the stage to address the public. Try to go through the whole chain two or three times and see if all the points fit in properly. If you have gone through the whole chain and revised all the points properly, you will remember them all.

□

7. LEARNING AND REMEMBERING

This chapter gives more insights on FRT and memory enhancement techniques. It explores further some frequently asked questions such as how can we remember better, what is the effect of time on memory etc. The chapter is designed for quick reading. It is suggestive rather than introspective. However, details are provided wherever required.

- **We always remember the initial chapters of any subject more than the middle and final chapters.** It is observed that, under normal circumstances, when a student starts a fresh academic year, he is focused in his work, because he is doing it after a break. Suppose the academic year ends in April and the next year begins in June, the subject matter taught during June and July is remembered better due to initial enthusiasm. Enthusiasm diminishes as the year progresses.

Also, every time we start studies and especially revision, we start with the first chapter. If we grow lax about regular studies or revision the later chapters are not studied. The first few chapters are also studied during half-yearly examinations. The later chapters are studied only once. Surveys show that for the so-called average students and those who barely pass, most of the marks are scored from material in the beginning the book. This teaches us to pay special attention to the final chapters of the book which are revised the least number of times.

- It is a good habit to read a chapter at least once before it is taught in class. It is a fact that **if we already know what is being taught in class, our attention improves**. The reasons are:

  (a) The desire to verify whether what we have learnt is correct.

  (b) If the teacher asks a question, we know the answer. This gives confidence.

(c) The teaching in the classroom is revision for a student who has read the material. We can see what we misunderstood when reading.

(d) Any concept that is first self-learnt and then learnt from a teacher is better understood than the other way round.

- Liking for a particular subject is directly related to liking for the teacher. If you like the teacher, you like the subject and if you do not like the teacher you do not like the subject.

- Understanding is the basis of remembering. Every year we are taught something about a subject. The next year we are taught something more about that subject. So, understanding is linking the old and the new together and forming a new picture. An effort should be made to learn the fundamentals of any subject, because that is what is going to be of help throughout our lives when most of the details will have been forgotten. The question is that if we read a lot of reference material will it help in understanding or will it confuse. **If you have understood the basics of any subject, extensive reading will prove helpful and not confusing.**

- Familiarity of something being learnt and similarity to something already known helps remember better.

- Forgetting is very rapid in the beginning and then becomes slower. Take a look at the figure shown below:

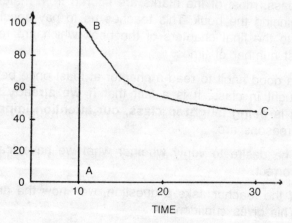

On the y-axis we have memory level and on the x-axis we have time. We see that the greatest amount of material is forgotten in the first few days after it is learnt. After that, we forget the subject matter slowly. Our memory level never reaches zero because we never forget all of what we have learnt. At least the principal, fundamental part is remembered for a lifetime. Suppose you have been taught Newton's third law of motion 'every action has an equal and opposite reaction'. You have understood that a rocket follows the same principle. Even the mechanism of the rocket is explained to you. As time passes, you may forget the mechanism of the rocket but you will always remember that 'every action has an equal and opposite reaction.' It is almost impossible to forget basic principles.

Remember that, as we saw in NRT/FRT, a person who is at point C in the above diagram will reach point B (maximum memory level) more easily than a person at point A. **The fundamental knowledge that is never forgotten enables a person to quickly and easily re-study the forgotten subject matter.**

EXTRA-LEARNING
'A Talent is never forgotten'

Once you learn how to fly kites, you never forget how to fly kites. Once you learn how to multiply numbers, you never forget it. You may forget the definition of standard deviation in statistics, but you will never forget how to divide a number by another. Why is it so?

One of the reasons why all these things are not forgotten is that they are learnt repeatedly. You have learnt them over and over again. Why is it that we never forget the songs of films or nursery rhymes, but we forget the poems taught in school? Why is it that the alphabet is never forgotten? Multiplication tables are also not forgotten.

They are not forgotten because they have been repeatedly used. When a child going to nursery school is taught A, B, C, D for the first time, it is as alien to him as any foreign language is to us. But with repeated learning and regular use the alphabet is internalised. The grown-up child automatically recollects the alphabet.

If a primary school child is playing a video game and you ask him to say the multiplication table of eight, he will pause the game, make an effort to remember and then say the table. An adult would continue playing the video game and say the table at the same time. The data '8 x 1 = 8, 8 x 2 = 16, 8 x 3 = 24...' **does not require complete attention to recall.**

When I solve sums of derivatives and integration, I have to constantly refer the formulae chart, but my mathematics teacher does not need to. For her, the reproduction of the formulae is automatic. **Due to continuous use (extra-learning) it has become an essential part of her fundamental knowledge-stock.** She has been teaching and practising (learning again and again) these formulae and so she will never forget them.

As you learn anything again and again and practise it, it is more and more firmly etched in your mind. A time comes when you need no further revision and whatever you have learnt becomes unforgettable.

Do you read and practice the alphabet at this age? Obviously NO. Because you simply know it. Similarly when you extra-learn anything frequently by continuous practice, it will be a part of your fundamental knowledge-stock and you will not need to learn it again.

This concept should not be mistaken for blind memorising or learning by rote. I am strongly against rote learning.

❏❏

8. TIPS FOR EXAMINATIONS

All of us take various examinations and tests throughout the year. They assess how much we know. We may think that we know everything or that we are the best but the proof will lie in our results. We need to learn the techniques which increase our efficiency in the examinations.

The examination techniques can be learnt under four headings.

- Primary Requirements
- Before the exams
- During the exams
- After the exams

PRIMARY REQUIREMENTS

There are three primary requirements that are a must in order to succeed in any exam. These three primary requirements are perfect preparation, a burning desire to succeed and skill in examination technique. We shall have a look at them one by one.

PERFECT PREPARATION

You cannot leave studies to the last moment. You *must* be regular in your work. There is no other way. Whatever techniques you learn will be useless, unless you are ready to put in regular effort.

It is your daily, regular effort that will bring you success. Organise your time in such a way that you give maximum priority to studies. No moment should go unutilised. Plan your work and spread it throughout the period between two examinations so that your time, energy, attention, etc. remain under your control.

You should know which chapters are assigned for the

examination, and what their weightage (marks allotted) is, which questions are compulsory and which are not, etc.

Perfect preparation does not come easily. You must study everything in the relevant part of the syllabus. You cannot leave out anything. There should not be a single question that you are unable to answer. It is such a nice feeling when you can answer any question about the material in your textbook. Have you ever tried it? You can try it now. Study a small chapter or a lesson thoroughly. Ask your friends or relatives to ask you any question based on that chapter. Feel the joy of being able to answer even the most difficult and tricky questions.

The second primary requirement is

A BURNING DESIRE TO SUCCEED

There are students who do not want to do very well in examinations. This is not a printing mistake. I repeat—there are students who do not WANT to do very well in examinations. How can you expect them to do well? You can never achieve what you do not want. Here in India, passing marks for most examinations are 105 out of 300. If you get 105 marks you are promoted to the next standard. There are students who do not wish to get even 110. They simply do not bother about getting 110. They say that if they get 105 it is enough and they do not desire more. They just want to scrape through. A strong desire is a prime requirement. You must have the desire to become outstanding.

I have a friend called Ankit who was a good student. He used to put in limited efforts and scored reasonably good marks. Once, he had a challenge with his friend that he would get more than 85 per cent marks in a particular examination. His friend was sure that Ankit would lose the bet. Since Ankit had accepted the challenge, it was a question of his self-esteem. He had to get the marks. He started working hard. Every day, his friend would remind him of his challenge and would laugh at him. This made him work even harder. He went on putting in more and more effort everyday. He had only one aim in mind and that was to cross the barrier of 85 per cent. His parents could not believe the sudden change they saw in him. **EIGHTY-FIVE PLUS** that was the only thing that kept ringing through his mind all day long.

Ankit scored 87.5 per cent and topped all the classes. The entire staff of teachers including the principal in his school - St. Xavier's - was stunned. The students who generally topped could not believe it. Everybody except for Ankit was surprised. This happened when Ankit was in standard eight. He had always considered himself to be an above average student but never a genius. He needed a spark of belief. He wanted an event to give him some sort of faith in his own potential. And that event had happened. From that day onwards there was no looking back. From then on, Ankit always topped the class in school. He always worked as if someone had challenged him to do an impossible job. He soon became used to getting the first rank. His brain had accepted the fact that he could always do it. He acquired a habit of success.

Shyam was giving his final year engineering examination. In his first attempt, he failed. In that year, there was no student in the whole state who had passed. All students had failed. Shyam was very disappointed. His family and friends told him that it was not a disgrace since everyone had failed. But, he did not want any sympathy. The next year he worked terribly hard. No other activities seemed to have any importance but his work. He used his capacity to the fullest. When the results were announced, there was only one student who had passed in the whole state. And it was Shyam.

I have given you real life examples of Ankit and Shyam where the goal to be achieved was difficult. But one thing was common in both the examples, and that was, a burning desire to succeed.

To succeed you must want to succeed. You must shun negative thought. You must have determination and confidence in yourself. This is a primary requirement.

SKILLS IN EXAMINATION TECHNIQUES

There was a survey in India of the students who generally perform well in examinations. The survey took into consideration examinations requiring descriptive answers, that is, a good deal of writing. The students were divided into three categories:

Students who were:

(1) Excellent in studies
Excellent in presentation and handwriting

(2) Excellent in studies
Average in presentation and handwriting

(3) Average in studies
Excellent in presentation and handwriting

When their results were analyzed, it was found that Category 1 scored the highest marks followed by 3 and then 2. It shows the importance of handwriting and presentation. Presentation skills scored above knowledge. Students who presented knowledge better scored more than their colleagues who knew more.

Imagine yourself from the moderator's point of view. You have to check many papers every day after the examinations. You must assess every question, write down question marks, add them up, check the total, enter it in the necessary papers, etc. They have to carefully observe every word and sentence that you have written and under such circumstances if they find it difficult to understand what you have written, they are not likely to give you good marks.

I once asked a senior moderator how they set the question papers. He said that every year they see the students' performance on individual questions in each subject. The question that the majority of students could not answer satisfactorily is repeated the next year. This may not be the general practice, but gives an idea of how question papers are set.

REMEMBER

- Solve previous year's papers for the exam you are taking.
- Time yourself.
- Get the papers corrected only by authority.
- Don't resort too much to 'Imp's.'

BEFORE THE EXAMS

Your mental state a day before the examination is something that you are going to carry with you the next day to the examination hall. So, don't stress yourself or overwork because it won't help. Harry Maddox has written a book called 'How to Study'. He says:

> 'If you have got behind your work it is usually better to concentrate on essentials and to make sure that you understand at least some of the ground work rather than to attempt to master the whole and to be left confused and to have only partially understood a mass of ideas.'

Don't study at the cost of sleep. A minimum of 6-7 hours of sleep is necessary before the examinations, because a drowsy brain cannot think. A fresh brain generates ideas! Avoid excessive study. I know of a girl who slept for just about 3 hours during her important examinations. There were six papers throughout the week. She used to only sleep for the least time possible. She wrote five papers well, but while writing her sixth and ultimate paper – geography - she went completely blank in the examination hall. Her brain simply refused to work. Nothing could help. The girl's eyes were filled with tears. No matter what she tried, she just couldn't carry on. She failed in geography.

Get yourself organised beforehand. Buy all necessary stationery. Fill ink in your pens; sharpen your pencils, etc.

Don't be anxious. Be confident. God is always with you. Believe in him. You may worry that you don't know the subject properly, but anxiety won't help. It will only increase the intensity of the problem. A little anxiety makes you alert and is desirable. But anxiety should not overpower you.

THE FINAL LINKS

As explained in the chapters dealing with memory, you should have a logbook of the chains and links which function as memory aids. Just go through them individually in detail. Because they represent the whole text material itself, you will be learning the whole of the chapters themselves just by studying the links. Also, if you are thorough with the links, it will greatly help you present the answers in the examination papers in a neat format. The advantage of the chain method is that the facts will occur in order of importance. If you just memorise the points, you may forget their order.

DURING THE EXAMS

As you sit down to write your paper, remember the technique of meditation for concentration. The coin in the bucket of water can only be seen when the water is calm. As you sit down for the examination, just sit back straight and close your eyes. Try to see the beauties of nature. Imagine a beautiful natural landscape full of beautiful flowers in blossom. Imagine diving inside a blue, pond and seeing colourful fish. All your tension, frustration and worry are dissolved in the water. See a rabbit running down a lush green meadow. View the innocent butterfly, the sun shining bright and a beautiful rainbow. If you are feeling nervous, then continuously say to yourself RELAX. You can say that,

'I am completely relaxed. I am calm and quiet.
I am feeling light and I love this situation.
I have no fear or nervousness of any kind.
I am at peace. Eternal peace is ruling me.'

This meditation will take not more than three minutes, but it will surely calm down all the emotions of anxiety, fear and worry. This will greatly **enhance your power of recollection**. The deep silence will reduce the chaotic activity of your brain. Pray to God to help you score good marks.

Organise your stationery around you and get ready to have the paper in your hand. After getting the paper in your hand, don't start writing immediately. Instead read all the questions. If you don't find the most expected questions, don't let it worry you. After reading the entire paper, start writing.

- Read carefully, don't misread.

Read again what is written in the box. Does it read *Paris in the spring*? Yes. You may be correct. But, does it really read *Paris in the spring*? Yes, you are very sure. But I am not. You will think it very foolish on my part to keep on asking you to do something as stupid as this, but there is a reason for it. Read it again: Does it still read, 'Paris in the spring'?

Yes, it does. Actually, it does not. The sentence reads 'Paris in the the spring.' Just see for yourself how careless you were. Casson has used it in his book to show people how to enhance their observation. The little x under the sentence is just used to bring the focus of the eye downwards.

Don't misread. Be careful while you read the paper. A question may be framed in a familiar manner. But there may be a slight change which alters the meaning of the question and hence the answer.

Another example is:

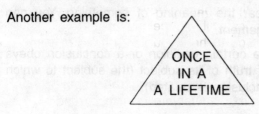

Read the sentence carefully.

It reads 'once in a a lifetime' and not 'once in a lifetime'.

Since you know the intention of putting this sentence over here, you will look at it properly but many people make a mistake when they look at it without the warning you have had.

There are specific words used in questions that demand a special form of answer from the student. Given below is a list that can help. I adapted this list from a book *Learning More Effective Study* by C. Bird and D. M. Bird. Each word used in the question demands a certain type of answer. It is important to understand the objective behind the use of a specific word.

Compare: List the similarities and differences.

Contrast: Set in opposition in order to bring out differences.

Criticise: Give your judgement or opinion along with evidence.

Define: Set down the precise meaning of a word or phrase.

Describe: Give a detailed or graphic account.

Discuss: Examine by argument and debate. Give reasons about the positive and negative factors.

Evaluate: Talk about the worth of something keeping in mind its truth and utility. Give less of your personal opinion.

Explain: Substitute the technical language with simple terms. Show how one thing leads to another (the cause and effect relation).

Illustrate: Use a figure or a diagram to explain or give examples.

Interpret: Make clear the meaning of something. You can give your own judgement.

Justify: Show that a certain decision or a conclusion obeys the general laws of truth of its subject (the subject to which the decision or conclusion is related).

Outline: Give the main features or general principles of a subject. Omit the minor details.

Relate: Show how things are connected to each other.

State: Present in clear brief form.

Trace: Follow the development or history of a topic from some point of origin.

After meditating regularly, you will probably enhance your intuition. You can use it to write your paper. Assume that you are stuck at a particular objective type question that has alternatives and you do not know the answer. Write the question without the answer, and proceed with the other questions. Forget about the question you cannot answer. You will find that when you are not thinking about that question, the answer will come to you unbidden. It is quite likely to be correct. This is because your mind subconsciously worked on the problem even as you wrote other answers.

AFTER THE EXAMS

After the exams, you cannot do much about increasing your marks. But you can definitely do something else. When your results are announced, carefully analyse your paper. Find where you made mistakes and where there is scope for improvement.

□□

9. A TALK WITH A MODERATOR

Given below, is my interview with Mr. P. Sharma, a moderator of the Maharashtra State Board of Education. It is very important to consider the opinion of the moderators, as they are the people who are going to check our papers and give us marks. Although every human being has a different style of assessing a given paper, there are certain common points and ideas that the moderators always consider essential to an ideal paper.

I did not have a formal interview, but a very informal talk. I have written his opinions, but not verbatim.

It is sometimes not possible for a moderator to go through the individual details of all the answers, especially in long answers. Moderators correct a large number of papers before a given deadline. It is impossible to read every word that every student has written. Moderators look for **keywords and phrases**. It becomes easier if the student has underlined them in the paper. If the jargon (terminology) is present, we can conclude that the student has done his work. For example, in an economics paper, a student who has done little work will use the word 'income' in his answer but a student who has put in more effort will use the words 'money income' and 'real income' in the correct places. Income is a common word and anyone can use it, but a student who has understood his economic concepts will know the difference between real and money incomes.

The reason for this is that education is a process of making professionals and moderators expect the student to know the terminology of a subject. Even if a student has explained the concept but is unable to use the right terminology, there is a reluctance to give him marks. Thus, it is very important to write the key words and the technical details of the subject that are mentioned in the textbook.

Another thing moderators look for is the orderly presentation of ideas. There is always a proper format for writing an answer. The format varies from subject to subject. For example, while writing a science experiment, the order is: the aim, the apparatus, the diagram, the procedure, the observation and finally the conclusion. Imagine how clumsy and senseless it looks if the conclusion is written before the observation. Similarly, there are logical orders for other subjects too. Sometimes a definition appears in the middle of a paragraph, which according to me is wrong. A definition or a quote should always stand out from the surrounding text. When a student jumps from one idea to another and then comes back to the original idea again, it shows that he is writing without adequate practice. The points should always be written in a descending order of importance. The most important point comes first and then the next most important. Sometimes, students draw a diagram and then write assumptions and explanation of the diagram together. However, an ideal answer has the assumptions before the diagram and explanation after it. Every subject has a specific structural pattern of answering. Remember, **a good answer properly structured will fetch more marks than a better answer badly structured.**

The initial or the first answer in a paper has a lot of importance. If the first answer is written very well and is capable of fetching good marks then all the subsequent answers will also fetch good marks. It is always said that the first impression is the final impression. If you think from the moderator's perspective, you will realise that if the first answer in a paper has a lot of cancellations and mistakes, a very low opinion is formed about the student and it is very difficult to overcome that opinion. A badly written first answer will not only fetch average marks but the subsequent answers will also have to pay a penalty. Try to do your best on the first answer.

Write the objective answers first and then the longer descriptive or subjective answers. As you start writing the examination, your speed of recollection is low. You gather speed as you write. Halfway through, your brain is at the maximum level of performance. Suppose you have a 100 marks paper to be written in 2 hours. This implies that on an average you should write 25 marks worth in every half an hour. Generally students are unable to complete more than 15-20 marks worth of paper in the first half-hour, but still manage to complete the entire paper in the stipulated time period. This suggests that the performance of the brain increases during the examination. You may write 30-35 marks' worth in the 3rd or 4th half-hour.

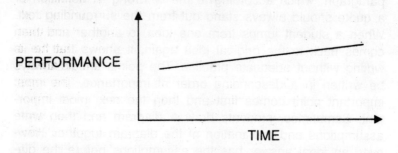

PERFORMANCE

TIME

Remember, it is always advisable to start writing your exams with the simpler problems and gradually move on to more difficult ones.

Handwriting and presentation are vital to success. There is always a tendency to give good marks to a well-presented paper. **What the eyes like the mind also likes.** A paper with a beautiful handwriting and presentation though without very good answers is likely to get good marks. Some moderators feel that extremely bad handwriting shows that the brain is in a state of panic and hyperactivity which is a sign of inadequate preparation and lack of self-confidence. A student who is composed and calm, who has prepared well has no need to panic or get frustrated. His preparation and confidence shown is seen in the paper in the form of good handwriting.

Originality in an examination is as important as the question makes it. In physics, chemistry and biology you need to write general laws and proven theorems. Many students write answers from 'study guides' and other supplementary material available in the market. As long as the answers match the questions, there is no harm in it. However, sometimes students rely too much on these sources of information. Mr. Sharma says, "Once, I was checking the English papers of a certain class in which they had to write an essay on 'An Hour at the Railway Station.' A student had written a very beautiful essay but I knew it had been extracted from a book. Thus, in my eyes the student was unworthy of getting marks. Even for topics like essays, letters and stories if you copy from study guides without using the slightest bit of originality, you do not deserve marks."

He discussed some other important points.

- As far as possible write answers in the same order as in the question paper. Try not to write the answers in a random order. It is feasible and easy to check a paper written question by question. Students should always try to write all answers together in a continuous fashion one after another rather than writing them in a haphazard manner. If a student frustrates the moderator by making his task tedious, he has less chances of getting good marks. This happens mainly in long papers.

- Never write rubbish. Length of answer is an important criterion for consideration but do not repeat the same point twice in different words just to increase the length of the answer.

- Suppose an answer has four parts - definition, explanation, advantages and disadvantages. It is necessary to give sufficient details of all four parts rather than writing two or three of them in excessive detail.

- Also, **the number of points that are written for any answer should be in the multiples of the marks allocated for the specific answer.** For example, if you are asked to distinguish/differentiate between tropical climate and equatorial climate and the marks allocated to the answer are 3, then the number of points that you should write are 3, 6, 9 etc. If the marks allocated to the answer are 4, then the number of points that you should write are 4, 8 etc.

A very good idea in a paper is capable of fetching good

marks when seen for the first time. But, as the moderator keeps on seeing the same idea in many papers, the idea loses its value and fetches fewer marks. Mr. Sharma gives an example. In an English examination, a student had written a good essay which ended with a beautiful sentence,

'Sweet memories are like an oasis in the desert sands of time.'

This sentence impressed the moderator so much that he gave the student 8 marks on 10. But, after correcting a few papers, he found the same sentence in another paper. This time he gave the student only 6 marks even though the rest of the essay was better than the first student's essay which had got him 8 marks. He found the sentence in a few more papers; the next two papers got 6 marks and the one after that 5 marks. The value of the sentence had diminished in his eyes. Later he found out that a tutor had dictated this sentence to a batch of students. He adds that this could happen with any moderator. Probably this is what happens when students try to copy ideas from external sources rather than thinking for themselves.

Mr. Sharma gives the example of the law of conservation of energy. This law is explained in the 7th and 8th standard textbooks. The 8th standard book gives more details than the 7th standard book. If an 8th standard student writes an answer on the basis of 7th standard knowledge, he will not get good marks. The purpose of education is to take you to the core of the subject as you advance to higher level of studies.

Mr. Sharma's opinions are not applicable to every examination structure. Different education boards have different approaches. Developed countries have a more practical approach than developing countries. There is also a 'human factor' so that the same answer may get more marks from one examiner and less from another. Assessment of multiple-choice questions does not have this human factor, then questions requiring descriptive, long answers does.

▭

10. USING MENTAL ABILITIES

A priest wanted people to understand the power of auto-suggestion. He called up a lady and told her, "Close your eyes and affirm for 5 minutes that you have a headache." The woman did exactly as she was told. She kept on repeating, "I have a headache." After a few minutes she really had a headache. She could feel the throb in her head. Said the priest, "When people think for just five minutes, that they have a headache, they really develop a headache. Think what will happen to people who have believed for the past 10-15 years that they are fools!"

If you think you are a fool you will surely turn into one.

This is **autosuggestion**. Thinkers such as Sigmund Freud, Jose Silva, Carl Jung, Dr. Maxwell Maltz, Shakti Gawain, Joseph Murphy etc. have written on this subject. Autosuggestion can make or mar your life. It can reduce a genius to a fool. It all depends upon what you think. Once you control your thoughts, your destiny is in your hands. You can get whatever you want - success, peace, fame, wealth, happiness, health, anything you desire.

We will study two techniques of controlling and using our mental processes for success – visualisation and subconscious study.

VISUALISATION

Visualisation is the technique of using imagination purposively. It is something that we have been using right from childhood but subconsciously, to create a feeling of pleasure or to forget painful experiences. As adults we can use it consciously to guide our thoughts and actions, and thus control our destiny.

IMAGINATION

In visualisation, we use our imagination to focus on an idea or mental picture regularly, giving it positive energy and affirmation until it is realised.

In her book *Creative Visualisation*, writer Shakti Gawain has explained the alpha and omega of creative visualisation. She has written many bestsellers including the book *Living in the Light*.

Thoughts lead to actions. Before we do anything, we think of it. For example, before we eat, we think of eating. Before we walk, we think of walking. A builder has a blueprint before he starts construction. An artist sees the picture in his mind, before he paints it. Everything which is created, is first created in the form of a thought.

Positive thoughts result in positive situations, circumstances, people etc. So the more positive energy we put in our thoughts, the more positive results we obtain in our lives.

HOW TO USE VISUALISATION?

Sit down in a quiet place. Be comfortable. Relax your body completely. Try to relax every part of your body. When you breathe in, try to breathe in positive, fresh and vibrant thoughts and feelings; when you breathe out, try to exhale negative thoughts and feelings. After some time, you will start feeling light and buoyant. At this stage start a countdown from 10 to 1, with every count try to feel more and more relaxed. When you feel completely relaxed, start to imagine something, as you want it to be.

For example, you want to get exceptionally good marks in any subject. Try to visualise yourself standing inside your classroom and your class teacher announcing that you have got the highest marks in that particular subject. You may **see** any other details that make it more real to you. Have fun with it. It should be an enjoyable experience.

Take care not to be too attached to the outcome. Don't pressurise yourself to achieve what you want. Just leave it to God. If you are too attached to your desire, you will only find disappointment. In his book *The Seven Spiritual Laws of Success*, my favourite author Dr. Deepak Chopra has given a Law of Detachment. He says that you must not be obsessed with what you want but should try to forget about it. Whenever you use visualisation to get anything, after visualising what you want, you try to forget it by saying some such words as, "I now leave my idea to God. I have faith that my prayer will be answered soon. I completely detach myself from the outcome.'

Bring your idea or mental picture often to your mind. Throughout the day whenever you think of it, give it positive energy. (To give positive energy is simply to believe that the thing will happen.) You will get what you want. Don't try too hard; just focus on it in a light and confident manner.

Visualisation will only work for good. You cannot use it to harm someone.

Visualisation can be of immense help in academic work. The meditation will create a silence and stillness in our minds that will sharply increase our ability to concentrate. Silence is of paramount importance to the ability to concentrate on anything.

There is another effective method of visualisation. Think of a screen, for example, a television screen. On that screen, visualise what you want in life. If you want to improve your relationship with someone, you can see it on that screen. You can visualise yourself shaking your hand cordially with that person or exchanging smiles. Make the picture colourful, lively and three-dimensional. View it for some time daily *just before going to sleep and just after waking up.*

If you are finding a particular chapter, problem, or any material in your textbook difficult to understand you can use the screen method. Visualise yourself able to solve all the problems under that particular chapter. Visualise it thrice a day for some time. One day you will find that you have got the answer to the problem or have understood the subject matter.

I use my own techniques for mathematics in my workshops.

One day, I was wondering whether I could ever reach a stage where I can do calculations at my mind. Yes, even without using a paper and a pen. I wanted to multiply a three-digit number by a three-digit number mentally. Let us say for example 248 by 963. I wanted to learn a technique by which I could multiply, divide, add, and subtract very big numbers mentally, without using paper and pen. I used the screen method of visualising. I saw myself giving a demonstration. There was liveliness, reality, colour and depth in my mental images. I carried the picture in my mind for about one week. Then a miracle happened. One day, I **dreamt** about some numbers in my mind. I do not recollect my dream exactly. But when I got up in the morning, I had got the solution to my problem. I thought of a system which can be used to calculate mentally. Even to this date, I use it in my seminars. (Now I can multiply and divide 4- and 5-digit numbers without using paper and pen.)

SUB-CONSCIOUS STUDY

According to Hindu legend, there was a time on earth when people possessed the wisdom and virtues of Gods. But the demands of physical life kept human beings from fully appreciating the gifts.

The creator of the universe, Brahma, concluded that it was wrong to leave such precious treasure lying unused. He decided to hide it where only the most persistent would ever discover it. There were suggestions to hide this gift deep under ground or at the bottom of the deepest ocean or on the highest mountain. Brahma rejected these suggestions because he believed man will find it in these places. "Let's hide it deep inside the people themselves. They will never think to look there."

And thus, for centuries, man has been wandering in vain in search of the gift, without appreciating that true enlightenment and bliss lie within his own inner self.

True knowledge, bliss and enlightenment lies within human beings. It lies deep, deep in our sub-conscious mind. The sub-conscious mind can be used for our studies too.

A study of the human mind is beyond the scope of this book. We will look for ways to use the sub-conscious mind in our work.

HOW TO PROGRAM THE SUB-CONSCIOUS MIND

When to ask?

You can ask your sub-conscious mind to give you what you want at any time. But, the best time is:

'Just before you go to sleep and just after you wake up.' Both the times you should be in your bed.

As soon as you lie down in your bed, you can ask your inner mind to give you what you want. Also, on waking up in the morning and while you are still in bed you can ask it what you want. These two are the best times and will give you the best results.

How to ask?

Asking means simply telling your inner mind what you want. If you want good marks, you have to simply affirm 'My sub-conscious mind is very powerful. It will help me achieve very good marks in my examinations. I have complete faith in its powers. I now leave the idea to my inner mind. It will work on my idea and give me results.'

- You can affirm anything that you want for about 3 minutes before you go to sleep and for another 3 minutes after you wake up. Do it regularly for a few days.

- You must feel peaceful and light-hearted when you affirm. Do not try to use power or force when you programme your inner mind.

There was a scientist called Friedrich Von Stradonitz, who wanted to arrange the six carbon and six hydrogen atoms to form the benzene molecule. He worked hard day and night but to no avail. All his efforts in vain. Finally, he decided to use his sub-conscious mind to solve the problem. He had faith in the workings of his inner mind and so he left the task entirely to his inner mind.

111

One day, he had a clear picture of a snake biting its own tail and turning around like a pinwheel. This image provided the clue to the circular rearrangement of atoms of the benzene ring.

You too can use your inner mind. There are various ways to do this.

(A) The Inner Mind As A Solution

Whenever you face a difficult problem, you can use your inner mind to solve it for you. You may find certain things difficult to understand, the inner mind/subconscious mind can come to your aid.

If you have any difficulty in, say, physics, just study as much of it as you can. Then, when you go to sleep at night, ask your sub-conscious mind to help you. After three or four days, read the chapter again and see how easy it appears.

Method

Lie down comfortably in your bed. Your room should be quiet and dark. Close your eyes. Try to breathe lightly and relax yourself completely. Allow 5 minutes for your body to relax. Then, just say for two to three minutes:

'I have infinite intelligence. God has made me a genius. I can easily understand everything. Nothing is difficult. My inner mind will help me learn the subject. I have full faith in its powers. I now leave the problem to my inner mind. I know my difficulty will be solved.'

There is no need to use the exact words, but the general idea should be to affirm confidence in the inner mind. Affirm twice a day for a few days and you will find that your problem is solved.

(B) The Inner Mind As A Helper

If you want to gain confidence in anything, your inner mind can come to your aid. It can help you remove negative-thoughts and unknown fears.

Method

Immediately after this exercise you must go to sleep, so do this exercise just before you go to sleep everyday. Choose a dark, peaceful room. Lie down comfortably in your bed. Close your eyes and concentrate. Try to feel light and full of energy. Try not to think of anything. Simply relax. JUST BE. After five minutes, slowly repeat the following lines with a feeling of joy,

'I am happy. Everything good is happening in my life. I trust God. He has always helped me in my life. He has always helped me in my studies. My brain is extremely sharp. I learn everything easily. This time I am going to do very well in my examinations. I have confidence in myself. My sub-conscious mind will help me gain confidence in life. I trust it.'

After having said these or similar words, you can go to sleep.

You can use your sub-conscious mind every day. What is required is just five to ten minutes of daily affirming. It will help you immensely in your studies.

After regular use, you will focus better on the material you study. Whenever you study, your attention will go to the right sections or the questions that are important.

You can also use affirmation to enhance your belief in your sub-conscious mind in general *if not for any* specific problem.

'My subconscious mind is listening to me. I am happy to have it as my guide. I am feeling a presence of success in my life. My life is perfect. I always achieve success in whatever I do. I have been infinitely blessed with success. Like a magnet, I attract success. The divine guidance is surrounding me. It is a perfect situation and I can experience it.'

After having said these words, just stay calm for two minutes and then resume your activities. Don't jump back to your work instantly after affirming. Stay calm for about two to three minutes. Breathe deeply and feel the positive en-

113

ergy of these thoughts. After a few minutes you can be ready to do your work.

There have been investigations in the West into subconscious learning. In one such study, an audio recording of a chapter from a textbook was played to students while they slept. The next morning, the students were asked to read that chapter. They learnt it far more easily than usual.

We have all been using only one part of our minds for our work, now we can use both the parts.

11. THE ULTIMATE CHALLENGE

How many of you believe that success is a matter of chance? If you believe that, I am afraid no one can help you. Luck may have a minor role in deciding our destiny, but it is nothing compared to the effect of confidence, determination and will. In this chapter, we will discuss habits that make people successful in life - successful on the strength of their own will, faith, and devotion towards work. It includes examples of people, inspiring ideas, motivating thoughts, proverbs etc. They are collected from various sources and largely reflect the ideas of success as described by great authors of our times.

CONFIDENCE

A teacher was teaching mathematics in two classes of the same standard. Let us say, the classes were A and B. Each class had 50 students. The teacher went to class A and gave a problem. She also told the class that the problem was so difficult that it took her two whole days do solve it. She also said that most students in class A would not be able to solve it.

She gave the same problem to the students of class B and told them that for homework she was going to give them an easy problem. She told them that all of them would be able to solve it without any difficulty.

When the students submitted their work, the teacher found that, in class A, 4 students had solved the problem and 46 had failed, while in class B, 46 students had solved the problem and 4 had failed.

The teacher was able to influence the attitudes of the students and thus their ability by a simple statement of expectation. It was not that the students who failed did not have the potential to solve the problem. Their negative approach got them a negative result. Their capacity was worthless without confidence.

We all know people who have failed in life despite being able, simply because they were influenced by the negative comments of the people around them.

Andrew Jackson said, 'One man with courage makes a majority.'

You must have seen the bumblebee. Now, the bumblebee has a very heavy body and a comparatively short wingspan. From the point of view of science, the bumblebee cannot fly. It is simply *impossible* for it to fly. But, the bumblebee does not know science! The question of not losing confidence does not arise. It just knows it must fly and so it does.

Ants can lift weights many times greater than the weights of their own bodies. Sometimes, they even lift up objects that are 50 times as heavy as their own bodies. According to biology, this is almost miraculous for any other specie of living beings to do. But once again, are the ants aware of this fact? No. They don't know it and so they just do it.

Confidence makes a big difference. Try to observe confident people. You will see a lot of energy, power and faith. We like their presence and knowing that these people are around makes us feel safe and secure.

If you think you are beaten, you are;
If you think you dare not, you don't.
If you think you like to win, but think you can't,
It's almost a cinch you won't.

If you think you'll lose, you're lost,
For out in the world we find,
Success begins in a fellow's will
It's all in the state of mind.

If you think you're outclassed, you are.
You've got to think high to rise,
You've got to be sure of yourself before
You can ever win the prize.

116

Life's battles don't always go
To the stronger or faster man;
But sooner or later the one who wins
Is the one who thinks he can.

— Walter D. Wintle

Some people never lose in life. You will find them continuously achieving more and more in life. They make the biggest and gravest difficulties appear very small by their mere confidence.

Someone has said, 'You can easily determine the caliber of a man by ascertaining the amount of opposition it takes to discourage him.'

A boy from a very poor family lost his father at a very early age. He had a young sister and a widowed mother to look after. The boy started working in his spare time. As time went on, he achieved more and more success in life. Despite facing many difficulties, the boy went on and on. One day in a party of business executives, someone asked him, "How come you achieved so much in life in the face of so many obstacles?" The boy said, "Kites rise against the wind, not with the wind."

You have to overcome difficulties to achieve success in life.

Napoleon Hill said, 'Every adversity has within it the seeds of an equivalent or greater benefit.'

LEARNING FROM FAILURES

'Failure is often God's own tool for carving some of the finest outlines in the character of his children.' — T. Hodgkin

Failure has been wrongly branded by society. Failure is viewed as though it is the end of the world. But as T. Hodgkin says failure is God's way of giving you courage, inspiration and determination to rise up.

'Our greatness does not consist in falling every time, but in rising every time we fall.' — Oliver Goldsmith

In the year 1952, Sir Edmund Hillary failed to climb Mount Everest. A few weeks after his attempt, a small gathering in England requested Hillary to address them. As he walked on the stage, there was a thunderous applause. People applauded because they appreciated the great attempt that Hillary had made. But, Hillary viewed himself as a failure. He did not consider himself worthy of the applause.

He moved towards a picture of Mt. Everest in a corner of the stage. He said, "Mount Everest, you beat me the first time….but I'll beat you the next time! Because you've grown all you were going to grow, but I'm still growing!"

The failure acted as a strong driving force that on May 29, 1953, Hillary became the first human being to conquer Mount Everest.

Many successful men of our times have failed some time or the other in their lives. I am not saying that failure is necessary in life. But failure can act as an incentive to try harder.

One day a teacher told his student, "Tom, you are too stupid to learn anything." Tom left school after just three months of formal training. His mother said, "My Tom is not stupid, I will teach him." That Tom became the great Thomas Alva Edison.

Albert Einstein never did well in school. His teachers were fed up with him. He was a very slow learner. This slow learner gave us the theory of relativity. It is regarded as one of the most complicated theories and the most difficult to comprehend. Einstein once said that there are only 12 living people who understand it although there are *more than 900 books attempting to explain* it. He was awarded the Nobel Prize for this theory. Years after his death, people marvel at a mind capable of producing such a theory.

'A smooth sea never made a skilful mariner.'

— Old English Proverb

Failure awakens the brilliance in us. We tend to take things more seriously. We give greater attention to the problem.

Not in the time of pleasure Hope doth set her bow;
But in the sky of sorrow, over the vale of woe.
Through gloom and shadow look we on beyond the years;
**The soul would have no rainbow, Had the eyes no
tears**.

— John Vance Cheney

All of you must have heard of the story of King Bruce and
the spider. King Bruce had lost a battle and he was afraid
that he would be taken captive by the enemy. He ran into a
forest and hid himself in a cave. Bruce was very tired and
had lost hope of regaining his position. In the cave, he saw
a spider trying to build a web for himself. The spider tried
several times and each time he failed. He rose up again,
and again he fell. But the spider did not lose courage. He
went on trying. Finally he succeeded and the web was built.
King Bruce, watching this, derived great inspiration from the
spider. He thought that if the spider could build a web after
having failed so many times, why could he not rebuild his
empire? A lost and tired Bruce rose up and said to himself,
"Now, I will rebuild my empire. Everything is lost but I still
have something with me - my confidence, my determination."

I know of a boy who never worked hard. He got very poor
marks in his examinations. One day he failed an examination. His father told him "Son, even though you have failed
this time, it is not the end of the world. You can view a
stone as a stepping-stone or an obstacle — it depends
upon you. The students who did better are no different from
you. They learn from the same teacher as you do. So, decide for yourself. If you study and get good marks you could
have your own business or get a good job. If you do not get
good marks once more, you can sit on the road and beg. It
is your destiny and you have to make it."

Many motivational speakers use the life story of Abraham
Lincoln as a classic example of what a human being can
achieve in the face of difficulties. When we read the story of
Lincoln's life, we wonder how such a man could become
one of the greatest American Presidents.

At the age of 7, his family was thrown out of the house and he had to work.
At the age of 9, his mother died.
At the age of 22, he lost a job as a stores clerk. He couldn't go to a law school.
At 23, he was in debt.
At 26 his business partner died and it took years for Lincoln to repay the debts.
At 39, he failed re-election to the Congress.
At 41, he lost his four-year-old son.
At 45, he lost the Senate elections.
At 47, he failed as the vice-presidential candidate of his party.
At 49, he once again ran for the Senate and lost.

And at the age of 51, this man became the president of the United States.

What is failure? It's only a spur

To a man who receives it right,
And it makes the spirit within him stir
To go in once more and fight
If you never have failed, it's an easy guess
You never have known a high success.

It's easy to laugh when the battle's fought
And you know that the victory is won;
Yes, easy to laugh when the prize you sought
Is yours when the race is run,
But here's to the man who can laugh at the blast
Of adversity blows; he will conquer at last;
For the hardest man in the world to beat,
Is the man who can laugh in the face of defeat.

— Emil C. Aurin

EFFORT

A board in a Swaminarayan temple reads,

There are six reasons why man reached the moon:

> EFFORT
> EFFORT
> EFFORT
> EFFORT
> EFFORT
> EFFORT

The birth of science for mankind took place when the stone age man rubbed two flint stones together to produce a spark of fire. On 21st July 1969, Neil Armstrong stepped on the moon. That was then one of the highest achievements of mankind. The credit does not go to the scientists of NASA alone. Every generation of mankind did its job; every individual did his part. It was not an individual victory or the victory of a nation; it was a collective victory of the human race.

There is no substitute for hard work. Vidal Sassoon said, 'the only place where **S**uccess comes before **W**ork is the dictionary.'

How doth the little busy bee
Improve each shining hour,
And gather honey all the day
From every opening flower!

— Isaac Watts

Effort is often seen in a negative light as something we are forced to do. 'Love your work and it will not be an effort'. Instead, you will want to do it. We have had a misconception of effort. If the desire emanates from our heart, work will be a joy.

'If one does not love work, one is always unhappy in life. In order to be truly happy in life, one must love work.'

— The Mother

121

'When work is a pleasure, life is a joy! When work is duty, life is slavery.'

— Maxim Gorky.

If you read the autobiographies of great men, you will find that all of them loved their work. They worked hard no doubt, but they worked hard with love and enthusiasm.

'The heights achieved by great men,
Were not achieved in sudden flight,
But while others slept;
They toiled upwards in the night.'

You will find that you have a natural talent towards certain types of work. You do some things better than others. In academics, you may love mathematics and science more than history or geography. Spiritual people call it their 'dharma'. If you make your career in the subjects you love, you will be successful. Pablo Picasso learnt to draw before he could talk. Picasso became a great painter. These early signs are signs of genius.

You will realise that sometimes when you do the thing you love, you lose track of time, and your enthusiasm and interest remain undiminished. Many great people who succeeded in their careers had a similar absorption in their work. If an artist and his work are separate, he cannot produce a good painting; but if the artist is lost in the world of his painting he will produce a masterpiece.

When Rabindranath Tagore composed poetry, no one dared to disturb him. Simply because, while composing poetry, he did not live in the material world. Even though he was physically present in the material world, he lived in his imagination in the world of poetry. He was awarded the 'Nobel Prize for Literature' for his work 'Gitanjali.'

One day Sir Isaac Newton was so lost in his work that he did not notice that his cat ate his dinner which his servant had left for him. When the servant returned to clear the plates, Newton told him he had yet to eat. The servant remarked that the plates were empty. "Oh, is that so," said

Newton, "then I must have eaten my dinner."

So if you want to succeed in life, 'Love your work. Be lost in it.'

'A duty which becomes a desire, will soon become a delight.'

— George Gritter

'If a man is a street sweeper, he should sweep streets as Michelangelo painted, or Beethoven composed music, or Shakespeare wrote poetry. He should sweep the street so well that even the hosts of heaven and earth will pause to say: here lived a great street sweeper who did his job well.'

— Martin Luther King, Jr.

Michelangelo's work won fame. He once said that if people knew how hard he had to work in order to gain his mastery, it would not seem wonderful at all.

Your efforts will be worthy only when

(a) You love your work
(b) You have a burning desire to succeed.

One man asked Socrates the secret of success. Socrates asked him to come to the river with him. At the river Socrates walked into the water asking the man to go with him. When the water rose up to their shoulders, Socrates caught the man by his neck and ducked him in the water. The man struggled, but Socrates was strong. After a few seconds, Socrates let him up. The man took a deep breath of air. At this moment, Socrates asked, "What did you want the most inside the water?"

The man replied, "Air."

Socrates nodded and said, "This is the key to success. When successes is as important to you as the air you needed, then alone will you get it. There is no other way."

When we face a 'must do' situation, our efficiency increases. Dora Albert has assigned special importance to urgent situations in her book *How to Cash in on Your Abilities*. Urgent situations make us work well. They force us to realise our potentials.

We see the phenomenon of the SSC examinations. Many students show a sharp improvement in performance from the ninth to the tenth standard. If they do not do well in the tenth standard, they do not get into a good college making it difficult to pursue a career of their choice. Students who never studied except at the last moment, become serious. It is a **'must do'** situation.

ATTITUDE

'Keep your face to the sunshine and you cannot see the shadow'

— Helen Keller

Maintain a positive attitude. Always look for opportunities in life and don't go around complaining that things are not going well. Your positive attitude will generate positive circumstances.

Two people looked at a glass filled half with water. One said it is half empty; the other said it is half full.

You must have all heard the story of David and Goliath. Goliath was a giant. He would challenge anyone to face him. No one dared to accept his challenge. People were afraid of his sheer size. A shepherd named David heard about Goliath and his challenges. People told him, "Goliath is too big to hit." David replied, *"No, he is not too big to hit, but he is too big to miss."* Saying so he hurled a stone at Goliath using his sling. Goliath was knocked down.

A paralytic confined to an armchair once decided to make a tour of his city. Many advised him to give up the idea, but nothing could dissuade him. He toured the city. On his return, one man asked him, "How could you do this despite the paralysis?'" The man replied, "The paralysis is in my feet, not in my brain."

When you change your attitude, even an obstacle becomes

124

an opportunity. Every failure shows the path to success. Read this folk tale from South-East Asia.

Many years ago there lived a priest in a village. He was the caretaker of an old temple built on a hill. Since, there was no one to help the old priest he used to do most of the work himself. Every day, he got up early in the morning and walked to a nearby stream to fetch water.

The priest carried a long stick over his shoulder and two pots were hung at the two ends of the stick. One of the pots had a small crack while the other pot was good. The pot with a crack lost half the water in it by the time he reached the temple.

One day, the cracked pot said to him, "Priest, I feel so ashamed of myself. I am good for nothing."

"Why?" asked the priest. "What makes you think so?"

"For a long time, I have been able to deliver only half the water that you fill in me. Because of the crack, half the water leaks along the way. You work so hard yet you do not benefit."

The priest pitied the pot and replied, "Tomorrow morning I want you to take a close look at the path we travel every day. You will be surprised to see what a boon you have been to me."

The next morning, the priest showed the cracked pot some beautiful flowers that had grown all along the path. The priest said, "I saw the crack and decided to use it. I planted seeds all along the way. Every day, while we travelled from the stream to the temple, you watered these seeds and you are continuing to water them. I have been plucking these flowers and decorating the main gate of the temple. If it were not for the crack, would I have got such wonderful flowers?"

In 1914, Thomas Alva Edison, one of the greatest scientists, at the age of <u>67</u> lost his factory worth a few *million dollars* in a fire. He had little insurance. The work of a lifetime was destroyed. He said, **"There is great value in di-saster. All our mistakes are burnt up. Thank God we can start anew."** Just three weeks after the disaster, he invented the phonograph!

Three men were working on the construction of a building. A man approached the first worker and asked him, "What are you doing?" The worker got angry, "Can't you see, I am applying cement over bricks." The man approached the second worker and asked him the same question. The worker replied in disgust, "I am erecting a wall." The man asked the question of the third worker. He said, "I am building a temple for mankind." Three workers, same work, same question, different attitude. One person was applying cement over bricks while another was building a temple for mankind.

Keep your attitude positive. Count your blessings. In all the examples above, you will find that these people refused to accept defeat. They had confidence in their potentials and their ability to achieve what the common man may term the impossible. If you are facing a difficulty, remember that there is the almighty to help you. Trust GOD.

'Faith is the bird that sings when the dawn is still dark.'

— Rabindranath Tagore

Remember, no event, no person, no situation, no circumstance, absolutely nothing in the world can beat you without your permission.

DON'T give them permission.

126

12. CONCLUSION

There is a reason why God has created you. There is a reason why you are living on this planet at this particular moment. God has given you a unique ability that he has not given anyone else on this planet. The creator has bestowed one unique talent upon you. No living person can beat you in that activity simply because you are the best in that.

An American businessman was once stranded on a deserted road in Saudi Arabia. His car failed and would not start no matter what he tried. Fortunately for him, a Saudi mechanic came along. He opened the bonnet of the car. Taking out a hammer from his bag, he hit something in the car ten times. On the tenth stroke, the car started.

"How much do I owe you?" the grateful American asked.

"A hundred dollars." said the mechanic.

"A hundred dollars? Oh boy, that is too much money. How do you justify your demands?"

"Simple" said the mechanic. "Ten cents for hitting ten times and ninety-nine dollars and ninety cents because I know where to hit."

Remember, knowledge is power.

The more you read the more you know. It is as simple as that. One of the factors on which your knowledge depends is how vast and how profound your reading is. If you are studying computers, then attend a computer class, think deeply, ask questions, discuss with your friends what has been taught every day, write down your thoughts, go to the lab and practice, consult your seniors, read the newspapers for information on the field, read books on the subject. Do everything you can. If you have any doubts write them down in your notebook and get them cleared. If you have a problem, do not rest until it is solved.

When you completely immerse yourself in your work, you do not leave any scope for failure. You know so much that you will always be in demand. 'Mastering text books' should never be your limited goal.

Keep abreast of the changes in your field. Initially our learning is restricted only to our textbooks. But as we progress, we must learn every moment. The whole world is our textbook.

I often criticised our education system. It was one of my favourite subjects. But some time ago, I realised that criticism was not getting me anywhere. Criticising will not solve the problem. I had to accept things as they were. Along with formal education, I started reading a lot of material that would help me write this book. Although this affected my studies then, it is proving of immense help now. Make the subject of your interest your sole purpose in life.

But the question is, 'How will you know for what purpose you were created? How will you know which is the activity you will perform better than anyone else?' The answer is very simple. Whichever work you love doing most is precisely the work for which you were created.

You must have a passion for doing it. Even if someone wakes you up in the middle of the night and tells you to do it, you must be ready to do it. Some people have a passion for music, while some have a liking for sports and the creative arts. Some have a strong liking towards medicine, others towards software. These are their 'purposes' in life.

Identify the one thing in life that you like most. Once you identify it, devote yourself totally to it. If you have a very strong liking towards medicine, it does not make any sense pursuing a career in MBA. Just because everyone is after MBA and we hear almost everyday that 'MBA is the future', 'management experts are going to dominate everyone' etc. It is not necessary to do what everyone else is doing. But, it is of the utmost importance to do what you like. Think about it before making a decision. Before taking a decision ask yourself 'Do I sincerely like it?' 'Am I capable of it?'

God has given you a particular talent in life. Identify and

nurture it. Allow it to blossom, and manifest so that you can spread its fragrance everywhere. If God has given you a natural talent in X, it is useless to pursue a career in Y. You are trying to do that work for which you are not created and you are trying to ignore that talent for which you have been created. Have you seen a great musician perform on stage? You will see that while he is performing his eyes are closed. His body movements are slight and he seems to be completely lost in his own world. He enjoys it. When an artist paints a picture of 16th century rural life, the whole village comes alive in front of his eyes. The people, the animals, the houses, the celebration, the festivals all become three dimensional in front of his eyes. Even when he paints for eight to ten hours continuously, he does not feel tired. His enthusiasm is not diminished. An artist never complains that he has to work hard for eight hours a day. In fact, he says that he has eight hours a day to enjoy himself.

When these people work, they completely detach themselves from the physical world. Immerse yourself in any one activity of life that you love most. Devote 100 per cent of yourself to it. If you devote 99.99 per cent of yourself, you cannot be sure of success.

In my neighbourhood, there was a small boy whose mother always complained that her son did not sit in one place when he studied. He would move around. His father also complained that his son had poor concentration. One day, the boy got a game of 'MECHANIX'. It had some plastic pieces of various sizes and some tools. The boy loved the game so much that for hours and hours he used to play with it. He made so many things that even his parents were stunned by the boy's creativity. He was totally engrossed in it.

The question is, did the boy have poor concentration or was unable to sit at one place as his parents complained?

Of course not. The difference was that now the boy was doing what he loved. Three to four hours a day the boy worked with the same enthusiasm. He became a mechanical engineer. His colleagues call him the 'ideas man' because of his creative ideas. Many years ago I had read a poster that said, 'Love your work and every day will be a holiday.'

How wonderful this idea is! Love your work and you will never get tired of it. No matter how much time you spend on it you will always want to do more. Can we say that Michelangelo worked hard for many hours on his sculptures? No, he did not work hard at all. He wanted to do it so he enjoyed it. The desire to do the activity emanated from his heart.

One morning at 9:00 o'clock, I met my friend Kunal in the college library. He was reading a book on physics. Kunal was so lost in his work that he never knew what was going on around him. I went away for some work. When I returned at around 5 o'clock in the evening, Kunal was sitting and reading the same book. He must have been there for more that 8-9 hours. "My God," I said, "You will die if you study so much."

Kunal said quietly, "Man, this is my life. I will die if I do not study physics."

Physics was his life. He lived it, ate it, slept it, played it. He enjoyed his work, enjoyed his life. No regrets and no complaints. His parents never told him to study physics. His teacher never asked him to. He wanted to do it himself.

The Brihadranyaka Upanishad says,

You are what your deep, driving desire is.
As your desire is, so is your will,
As your will is, so is your deed,
As your deed is, so is your destiny.

The problem with most people is that they have accepted the fact that life is just drifting around. They have mistaken petty achievements with great accomplishments. They just want to live as they are without even realising that there is more to life than they think.

There have been billions of people on this planet, but almost all of them lived a life of little accomplishment. It does

130

not make much difference that they lived. People remembered them for a few days after they died and then they were forgotten. But there were few, who changed the course of history. These great individuals have motivated whole masses of people. They have fiercely battled the challenges of life to rise among their fellow men, to leave their footprints in the sands of time.

These individuals are role models to the rest of us. Great personalities like Mahatma Gandhi, Abraham Lincoln, Mother Teresa, Lady Diana inspire others years after their death.

The only thing that separates them from us may be the fact that they believed in themselves. They said 'I can' and they did!

I often wonder why, in spite of the unlimited power that God has bestowed upon us, we rarely accomplish anything great. Most of us get up in the morning, go to work, eat twice a day and go to sleep. We should do much, much more than this. Don't think that I am stressing material accomplishments. Material accomplishments are temporary. One moment you possess all the wealth in the world and the next you don't. Running after material wealth does not get us anywhere. In fact, human wants are unlimited. Today, you want a cycle. Then when you get one, you want a motorbike. Then you want a car. Then you want two cars. This leads you to an unending cycle of possession. You want things partly as a status symbol and partly to 'show off.' You have to wear various social masks in order to maintain your illusory prestige.

You cannot be sure that tomorrow you will possess all those things that you have today. But your talents, your art, your character, your determination, are assets which never get exhausted. An individual cannot be great by amassing a huge amount of wealth but only by achieving skill and mastery in his field of pursuit. People like Leonardo da Vinci, Picasso, Amitabh Bachchan, Shakespeare, Sir Donald Bradman, Charlie Chaplin etc. have spent their whole lives with just one aim in mind, to achieve excellence in their field.

Have a goal in life and focus on it. Make it your life. Right now, while you are reading this book, close your fists tightly. Right now. As tightly as you can. Now take a deep breath. Look up at the sky and try to feel 'POWER.' Feel 'POWER' flowing through you. Now, affirm strongly 'I WILL DO IT. Yes. Yes, I will do it.'

And now look at the abundant sky above you.

It is throwing a challenge to you. The sky is infinite. It tells you 'RISE IN LIFE.' 'RISE.' Come to me.

The mighty sky is telling you to be a leader. To be the best in your work. To make it to the top. Decide. Decide at this moment. Decide right now what do you want to do. This moment is golden. This moment can be the

'NEW DAWN OF YOUR LIFE,'
It is this moment that counts.
Keep this book aside and decide for yourself.
Decide.
Right now.

BIBLIOGRAPHY

I not only recommend the following books to the reader but take this opportunity to express my gratitude to the authors for writing these books.

Carnegie, Dale: *How To Win Friends And Influence People*

Carnegie, Dale: *How To Stop Worrying And Start Living*

Carnegie, Dale: *How To Develop Self-Confidence And Influence People Through Public Speaking*

Chopra, Dr. Deepak: *The Seven Spiritual Laws Of Success*

Chopra, Dr. Deepak: *Ageless Body, Timeless Mind*

Chopra, Dr. Deepak: *Perfect Health*

Chopra, Dr. Deepak: *Creating Affluence*

Covey, Stephen: *The Seven Habits Of Highly Effective People.*

De Bono, Edward: *Lateral Thinking*

Dyer, Dr. Wayne W.: *Manifest Your Destiny*

Dyer, Dr. Wayne W.: *The Sky Is The Limit*

Gawain, Shakti: *Creative Visualization*

Gawain, Shakti: *Living In The Light*

Goldratt, Eliyahu: *The Goal*

Hill, Napoleon: *The Master-Key To Riches*

Hill, Napoleon: *Think And Grow Rich*

Khera, Shiv: *You Can Win*

Maltz, Dr. Maxwell: *The Magic Of Self-Image Psychology*

McCormack, Mark: *What they don't teach you at Harvard Business School*

Murphy, Dr. Joseph: *The Power Of Your Subconscious Mind*

Peale, Dr. Norman Vincent: *The Power Of Positive Thinking*

Peck, M. Scott: *The Road Less Travelled*

Redfield, James: *The Celestine Prophecy (A Set Of Books)*

Robbins, Anthony: *Unlimited Power*

Robbins, Anthony: *Awaken the Giant Within*

Schuller, Dr. Robert: *Believe In The God Who Believes In You*

Schwartz, David: *The Magic Of Thinking Big*

Silva, Jose and Burt Goldman: *The Silva Mind Control Method Of Mental Dynamics*

Silva, Jose and Philip Miele: *The Silva Mind Control Method.*

Books on speed and memory techniques

Jagadguru Swami Sri Bharati Krishna Tirthaji Maharaj: *Vedic Mathematics*

Cutler, Ann and Rudolph Mcshane: *The Trachtenberg Speed System of Basic Mathematics*

Lorayne, Harry: *How To Develop A Super Memory — Memory Makes Money Mind-Power*

Desraj: *How To Get Outstanding Success in Academic and Competitive Examinations*

Maddox, Harry: *How To Study*

Atthareya, N.H.: *Speed Reading*

Pitman, Isaac: *The Pitman's Shorthand Course*

Thakore, Abhishek: *The Portrait of a Super-Student*

QQ

'**AWAKE,**
ARISE
and
STOP NOT
TILL THE **GOAL** IS REACHED....'

— Swami Vivekananda

'AWAKE,

ARISE

— Swami Vivekananda